New Orleans parade

National Geographic's Driving Guides to America

Texas
And Louisiana, Mississippi, Arkansas, and Oklahoma

By Mel White
Photographed by Danny Lehman

Prepared by
The Book Division
National Geographic Society
Washington, D.C.

Credits

National Geographic's Driving Guides To America Texas and Louisiana, Mississippi, Arkansas, and Oklahoma

By MEL WHITE
Photographed by DANNY LEHMAN

Published by
THE NATIONAL GEOGRAPHIC SOCIETY

Reg Murphy
President and Chief Executive Officer

Gilbert M. Grosvenor
Chairman of the Board

Nina D. Hoffman
Senior Vice President

Prepared by The Book Division

William R. Gray
Vice President and Director

Charles Kogod
Assistant Director

Barbara A. Payne
Editorial Director

Driving Guides to America

Elizabeth L. Newhouse
*Director of Travel Books
and Series Editor*

Cinda Rose
Art Director

Thomas B. Powell III
Illustrations Editor

Caroline Hickey, Barbara A. Noe
Senior Researchers

Carl Mehler
Senior Map Editor and Designer

Staff for this book

Keith R. Moore
Project Manager

Barbara A. Noe
Text Editor

Suez Kehl
Designer

Thomas B. Powell III
Illustrations Editor

Carl Mehler
Senior Map Editor and Designer

Kristin M. Edmonds
Mark Fitzgerald
Sean M. Groom
Mary E. Jennings
Researchers

Paulette L. Claus
Editorial Consultant

Tracey M. Wood
Map Production Manager

Sven M. Dolling, Thomas L. Gray,
Keith R. Moore, Joseph F. Ochlak
Map Researchers

Jehan Aziz, Sven M. Dolling, Michelle
H. Picard, Tracey M. Wood
Map Production

Tibor G. Tóth
Map Relief

Meredith C. Wilcox
Illustrations Assistant

Richard S. Wain
Production Project Manager

Lewis R. Bassford
Production

Peggy J. Candore, Kevin G. Craig,
Dale M. Herring
Staff Assistants

Mark A. Wentling
Indexer

Thomas B. Blabey, Sheila M.
Green-Kenton, Justin Tejada
Contributor

**Manufacturing
and Quality Management**

George V. White, *Director*
John T. Dunn, *Associate Director*
Vincent P. Ryan, *Manager*

Cover: Chisos Mountains, Texas
CARR CLIFTON

Previous pages: Rock formation near
Castolon, Big Bend National Park, Texas

Facing page: Produce stand on Ark. 62,
near Garfield, Arkansas
Left: Alligator, Jungle Tour on Avery Island,
Louisiana

Contents

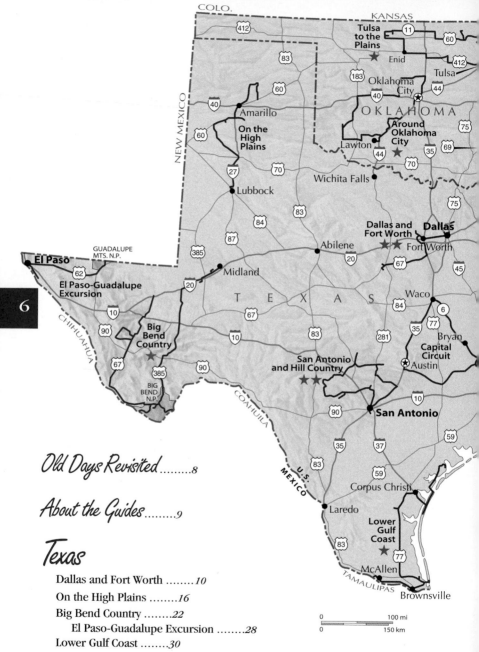

Old Days Revisited *8*

About the Guides *9*

Texas

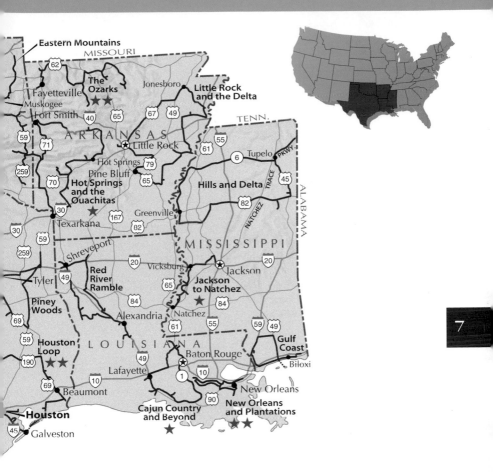

The summer I was seven years old, my parents packed up our yellow Pontiac and we headed west to visit my uncle and aunt and cousins in faraway Tucson, Arizona. My father had a deep aversion to driving through anything resembling a big city, so I recall the trip as a succession of neon-lit tourist courts in towns like Hope, Arkansas, and Shamrock, Texas. I remember, too, how I pestered my parents to stop at every roadside attraction we passed. I didn't want to miss a single rock shop or snake show between the Ozarks and the Painted Desert.

The journey had an enduring influence on my malleable young mind; for years, well into adulthood, I had dreams that were somehow related to that long-distance drive, and to all the wonderful new things I'd seen. And, even more, to the act of travel itself: the experience of cresting a hill and seeing undiscovered terrain, or of slowing down to pass through a town and getting a glimpse of the way people lived in someplace like Wichita Falls.

These days, with the fast-food strips that line the approach to every city, we all live a lot more alike than we used to. But enough differences remain that I still enjoy pulling into a new town and seeing what's up. If you feel the same way, I hope this book will lead you to undiscovered places—to some odd little museum, perhaps, beside a narrow grassy strip that once was a railroad track. Here's my advice: Ask the old fellow at the front desk to tell you a bit about the place, then sit back and listen. The stores in the malls may all be the same now, but every town's history is unique.

At full sail near Gulfport, Mississippi

Who knows? It could be that what I do for a living may be a direct consequence of that first cross-country trip back in the 1950s. It could be that the addictive anticipation I feel when I travel may just be a rekindling of what a wide-eye kid felt as he peered out through a car window and pointed and pleaded, "Can we stop here? Can we?"

When it comes to remembering things past, Proust can have his madeleine—I've got Cactus Carl's Reptile Ranch.

MEL WHITE

About the Guides

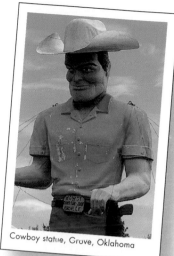

Cowboy statue, Grove, Oklahoma

*N*ATIONAL GEOGRAPHIC'S DRIVING GUIDES TO AMERICA invite you on memorable road trips through the United States and Canada. Intended both as travel planners and companions, each volume guides you on preplanned tours over a wide variety of terrain to the best places to see and things to do. The authors, expert regional travel writers, star-rate (from none to two ★★) the drives and points of interest to make sure you don't miss their favorites.

All distances and drive times are approximate (if you linger, as you should, plan on considerably more time). Recommended seasons are the best times to go, but roads and sites are open all year unless otherwise noted. Besides the stated days of operation, many sites close on national holidays. For the most up-to-date site information, it's best to call ahead when possible.

Then, with this book and a road map, set off on your adventure through this awesomely beautiful land.

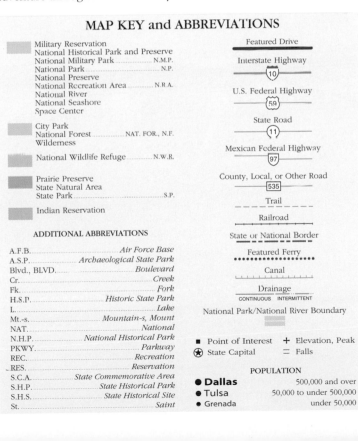

MAP KEY and ABBREVIATIONS

Military Reservation
National Historical Park and Preserve
National Military Park .... N.M.P.
National Park .... N.P.
National Preserve
National Recreation Area .... N.R.A.
National River
National Seashore
Space Center

City Park
National Forest .... NAT. FOR., N.F.
Wilderness

National Wildlife Refuge .... N.W.R.

Prairie Preserve
State Natural Area
State Park .... S.P.

Indian Reservation

ADDITIONAL ABBREVIATIONS

A.F.B.	*Air Force Base*
A.S.P.	*Archaeological State Park*
Blvd., BLVD.	*Boulevard*
Cr.	*Creek*
Fk.	*Fork*
H.S.P.	*Historic State Park*
L.	*Lake*
Mt.-s.	*Mountain-s, Mount*
NAT.	*National*
N.H.P.	*National Historical Park*
PKWY.	*Parkway*
REC.	*Recreation*
RES.	*Reservation*
S.C.A.	*State Commemorative Area*
S.H.P.	*State Historical Park*
S.H.S.	*State Historical Site*
St.	*Saint*

Featured Drive

Interstate Highway
(10)

U.S. Federal Highway
(59)

State Road
(11)

Mexican Federal Highway
(97)

County, Local, or Other Road
[535]

Trail

Railroad

State or National Border

Featured Ferry
•••••••••••••••••••••

Canal

Drainage
CONTINUOUS INTERMITTENT

National Park/National River Boundary

■ Point of Interest   + Elevation, Peak
★ State Capital   = Falls

POPULATION

● **Dallas**   500,000 and over
● Tulsa   50,000 to under 500,000
● Grenada   under 50,000

● **200 miles** ● **3 to 5 days** ● **Year-round** ● **It helps to study a map and know where you're going before tackling the maze of freeways in and around Dallas.**

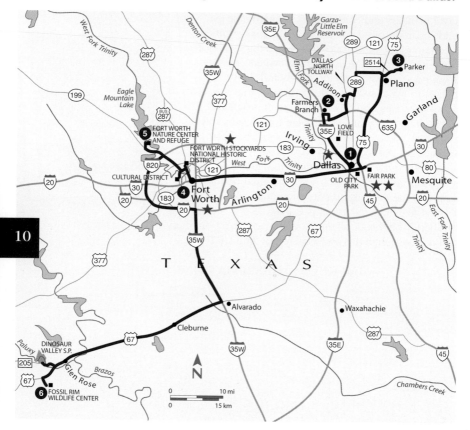

Short on mileage but long on attractions, this route stays mostly within the sprawling, seemingly endless metropolitan region of Dallas and Fort Worth, with an excursion at the end to see some honest-to-goodness dinosaur footprints. While it sometimes seems that nearly everything in the Metroplex (as locals call the area) was built in the last month or two, a number of fine historic sites endure amid the glitter, from an outstanding collection of art deco buildings in Dallas to Fort Worth's stockyards district, which combines the city's "cow town" past with a modern entertainment zone. Museums, too, highlight the drive, most especially Fort Worth's Kimbell Art Museum, among the nation's finest.

❶ **Dallas ★** *(Visitors Bureau 214-746-6677 or 800-232-5527)* rose up along the Trinity River in Texas' blackland

prairie region, its growth spurred by the arrival of the railroad in 1872 and the discovery of oil in East Texas in 1930. For a sky-high view of America's eighth most populated city, take the elevator to the 50th-floor observation deck of **Reunion Tower** *(300 Reunion Blvd. 214-651-1234. Adm. fee),* the ball-on-a-stick landmark on downtown's western edge.

For Americans of a certain age, the event that took place on nearby Elm Street on November 22, 1963, remains a tragic and indelible memory. The assassination of President John F. Kennedy is the focus of the **Sixth Floor Museum**★ *(411 Elm St. 214-747-6660. Adm. fee),* but the extensive exhibits here also recall his life and the impact his career and death had on the nation. Located in the old Texas School Book Depository building, on the floor from which Lee Harvey Oswald allegedly fired the shots that killed the President, the museum includes photographs, documentary films, the original corner window where Oswald knelt, and an FBI model of Dealey Plaza below.

Two blocks away stands the somber **John F. Kennedy Memorial** *(Main and Market Sts.),* designed as simple white walls surrounding a block of granite bearing Kennedy's name. Adjacent to the memorial are the 1892 **Old Dallas County Courthouse,** nicknamed "Old Red" for its red sandstone exterior, and the **Dallas County Historical Plaza,** with a log cabin modeled after one built by Dallas founder John Neely Bryan, who settled here in 1841. Just a bit farther north is the **West End Historic District** *(Bounded by Market,*

Dallas skyline

Record, and Ross Sts.), where restored commercial buildings now house restaurants, music clubs, and shops, making it one of the city's principal entertainment areas.

Texas School Book Depository, now the Sixth Floor Museum

The **Dallas Museum of Art**★ *(1717 N. Harwood St. 214-922-1200. Closed Mon.)* houses major collections of African, Asian, American, and Indonesian art, including contemporary paintings and sculptures, as well as antiquities. Most immediately striking is Claes Oldenburg's gigantic "Stake Hitch," dominating a room just off the museum entrance.

And speaking of oversize art... **Pioneer Plaza** *(Young and Griffin Sts.)* claims the world's largest bronze monument: A grouping of dozens of bigger-than-life longhorn cattle and mounted cowboys, depicting a moment from a typical 19th-century trail drive. South of I-30, **Old City Park** *(1717 Gano St. 214-421-5141. Closed Mon.; adm. fee)* comprises nearly 40 restored buildings from the years 1840 to 1910, relocated here from around the north Texas area. Among the highlights of this noteworthy historical attraction are a train depot, a Queen Anne-style house, a hotel, and a general store.

In 1936 Dallas hosted a grand celebration honoring the centennial of the Republic of Texas in **Fair Park**★★ *(1300 R.B. Cullum Blvd. at Grand Ave. 214-670-8400),* site of the annual State Fair of Texas. The structures remaining now constitute America's largest collection of art deco exposition buildings, as well as the nucleus of the city's most important museum complex. The imposing **Hall of State** *(3939 Grand Ave. 214-421-4500. Closed Mon.)* stands as a shrine to Texas history, with a monumentally columned marble hall dominated by a huge golden seal adorned by a central lone star. Among Fair Park's other notable sights: the **Dallas Museum of Natural History** *(3535 Grand Ave. 214-421-3466. Adm. fee),* with dioramas of the Texas environment and popular fossil displays; the **Dallas Aquarium**★ *(1st St. and Martin Luther King Blvd. 214-670-8443. Adm. fee),* featuring hundreds of species of fish and regular shark and piranha feedings; the **Age of Steam Railroad Museum** *(1105 Washington St. 214-428-0101. Wed.-Sun.; adm. fee),* with steam and diesel locomotives and restored Pullman cars; the **African American Museum** *(3536 Grand Ave. 214-565-9026. Closed Mon.),* comprising a large collection of art, artifacts, and historical displays; and the **Science Place** *(1318 2nd Ave. 214-428-5555. Adm. fee),* full of interactive exhibits on everything from optics to health to dinosaurs, with an adjoining planetarium.

In the northern suburb of ❷ **Farmers Branch,** the **Farmers Branch Historical Park** *(2540 Farmers Branch Ln. 972-406-0184)* contains an interesting set of historic buildings, among them an 1877 railroad depot, an 1856 stone dogtrot house, and 1840s log structures representing the period when many European immigrants settled in the area.

The **Cavanaugh Flight Museum** ★ *(4572 Claire Chennault Dr. at Addison Airport. 972-380-8800. Adm. fee)* in Addison offers aviation fans a remarkable collection of restored aircraft, including Warhawk, Mustang, and Spitfire fighters from World War II; a B-25 bomber that flew 83 missions in Europe; and an F-86 and Russian MiG-15 of Korean War age, early jets that now seem almost antique.

In the late 1970s and early '80s, millions of people around the world based their impression of Dallas on the television series of the same name, and so imagined a city populated by filthy-rich schemers and adulterers. In

❸ **Parker,** just east of Plano, stands the **Southfork Ranch** *(3700 Hogge Rd. 214-442-7800. Adm. fee),* the exterior site for J.R. Ewing's ranch and still a major attraction for fans of the show. In the nearby Visitor Center a museum displays show memorabilia.

Forever linked by a hyphen to Dallas, ❹ **Fort Worth** ★

Chisholm Trail mural in Sundance Square, Fort Worth

(Visitors Bureau 817-336-8791 or 800-433-5747) richly deserves the undivided attention of any traveler to the Lone Star State. Founded as an Army post in 1849, Camp Worth developed into a thriving city centered on stockyards, slaughterhouses, and meatpacking plants. Fort Worth's first century and a half is the focus of the exhibits at **Fire Station No. 1** *(2nd and Commerce Sts. 817-732-1631),* a 1907 firehouse converted into a museum of local history.

Only a block away, the **Sid Richardson Collection of Western Art** *(309 Main St. 817-332-6554. Closed Mon.)* displays paintings by renowned artists Frederic Remington

Fort Worth-style advertising

and Charles M. Russell, whose cowboys and Indians, dusty landscapes and big skies preserve a romantic Old West past. Housed in a Victorian-style building, the Richardson Collection is located in a historic district called **Sundance Square** *(Bounded by Calhoun, Throckmorten, 2nd, and 5th Sts. 817-339-7777),* now filled with restaurants, theaters, and shops. And while downtown, don't miss the dazzling **Water Garden** *(15th and Commerce Sts.),* 4 acres of waterfalls and pools.

Fort Worth proudly plays up its Old West heritage—nowhere more vividly than at the **Fort Worth Stockyards National Historic District** ★ *(N. Main St. and Exchange Ave.),* formerly a livestock-trading hub second only to Chicago in importance, now a lively entertainment center. The **Stockyards Visitor Information Center** *(130 E. Exchange Ave. 817-624-4741)* can provide guidance on the sights here, which include shops, restaurants, mule barns and cattle pens, and even a few saloons that rank as historic attractions in themselves. The adjacent 1902 **Livestock Exchange Building** *(131 E. Exchange Ave.)* still holds cattle sales; it also houses the **Stockyards Museum** *(817-625-5087),* with exhibits and memorabilia on the area's glory days. The 1908 **Cowtown Coliseum** *(121 E. Exchange Ave. 817-625-1025)* hosted the world's first indoor rodeo in 1917, and continues to host rodeos and shows.

The brightest star in Fort Worth is its **Cultural District,** a group of museums located within easy walking distance of each other west of downtown. Most renowned among them is the **Kimbell Art Museum** ★ ★ *(3333 Camp Bowie Blvd. 817-332-8451. Closed Mon.),* one of Texas' truly outstanding arts attractions. Though it likes to call itself "America's best small museum," there's nothing undersized about the collection; allow plenty of time to study works ranging from ancient Greek sculptures and a unique Maya stela to paintings by Picasso and sculptures by Miró.

Nearby, the **Amon Carter Museum** ★ *(3501 Camp Bowie Blvd. 817-738-1933. Closed Mon.)* began with a wealthy oilman's passion for the paintings and sculpture of Frederic Remington and Charles M. Russell, but has expanded its scope to encompass a wider range of American art: paintings by Thomas Cole, Mary Cassatt, and Georgia O'Keeffe, and an outstanding collection of photographs ranging from early daguerreotypes to works by Ansel Adams and Eliot Porter. Across the street, the **Modern Art Museum of Fort Worth** *(1309 Montgomery St. 817-738-9215. Closed Mon.)* creates a niche for itself by focusing on works by Picasso, Warhol, Rothko, and other notables of the modern era.

Old-line Eateries

The D-FW area boasts a wide assortment of restaurants in categories to match anyone's appetite, including some of the finest in the region. For a taste of the cities' traditions, stop in at two long-established favorites: **Sonny Bryan's Smokehouse** *(2202 Inwood Rd. 214-357-7120. Lunch only),* just south of Dallas's Love Field, where barbecued ribs and brisket scent the air with an incomparable aroma; and **Joe T. Garcia's** *(2201 N. Commerce St. 817-626-4356. Lunch and dinner),* a huge, rambling Mexican spot not far from the Fort Worth Stockyards. Though there are other locations of both establishments, these original spots have cooked up delicious memories for generations of local diners.

14

In contrast to those contemporary names, decidedly ancient creatures are a major attraction at the **Fort Worth Museum of Science and History** ★ *(1501 Montgomery St. 817-732-1631. Adm. fee):* Ever popular dinosaurs always attract a crowd, especially the dramatic display here of two of the long-vanished creatures (or their bones, anyway) in the midst of mortal combat. The museum also offers exhibits on the human body, rocks and fossils, and computers, as well as a planetarium and a surround-screen theater.

If your brain is suffering from overstimulation, find some peace nearby at the **Botanic Garden** *(3200 Botanic Garden Blvd., W of University Dr. 817-871-7686),* where you can wander though 110 acres of formal and naturalistic plantings.

For a primer to the region's natural environment, sample the trails at the ❺ **Fort Worth Nature Center and Refuge** *(9601 Fossil Ridge Rd., off Tex. 199. 817-237-1111. Closed Mon.),* northwest of town. Encompassing woodland, prairie, and bottomland along the West Fork Trinity River, the refuge's varied habitats create homes for equally diverse plants and wildlife.

Follow I-35W south to US 67 and turn west to Glen Rose, home of two quite different wildlife attractions. **Dinosaur Valley State Park** *(Off Rte. 205. 254-897-4588)* is a perfectly nice park, with the standard campsites and hiking trails—but, as its name implies, there's something more here. In places along the Paluxy River can be seen well-preserved footprints of dinosaurs that lived in this region more than 100 million years ago. The dramatic prints seem to show a huge plant-eating dinosaur being followed, perhaps stalked, by a smaller carnivore. Exhibits at the Visitor Center interpret the intriguing site.

Not far from this evidence of long-gone beasts roam exotic animals very much alive. ❻ **Fossil Rim Wildlife Center** *(Off US 67. 254-897-2960. Adm. fee)* is part drive-through zoo, part conservation center specializing in breeding endangered wildlife. Among the more than 1,000 animals found here are familiar giraffes and zebras, as well as lesser-known species such as red wolves, scimitar-horned oryx, and Attwater's prairie chickens. The center offers a variety of experiences, from a 9.5-mile auto route to guided tours to overnight trips modeled on African safaris.

Backtrack to US 67 to return to Dallas.

At the Botanic Garden

15

● **310 miles** ● **3 to 4 days** ● **Year-round**
● **Occasional cold fronts in winter can bring bitter winds and send temperatures plummeting.**

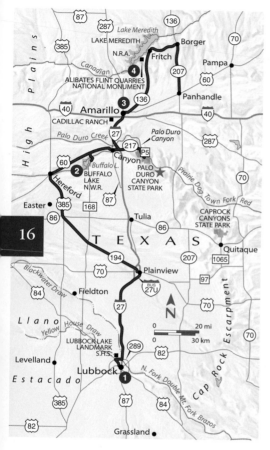

Take a look at some of the town names in this part of Texas—Levelland, Plainview, Grassland, Fieldton—and you might get an idea of the prevailing terrain. It's flat prairie here…in places, very, very flat. Gravel, sand, and clay eroded from the Rocky Mountains were washed out onto these lower lands millions of years ago, forming broad plains showing little relief, with few creeks to erode canyons or valleys.

The story goes that early Spanish explorers called this region the *Llano Estacado*—the Staked Plain—because the landscape was so featureless that travelers had to drive stakes into the earth to mark trails. Before settlers arrived to establish farms and ranches, it was a vast short-grass prairie of bison, pronghorn, and prairie dogs, where nomadic Native American tribes hunted. This is also, residents proudly point out, the region that built the state capitol in Austin. In the 1880s, Texas had huge expanses of land but little cash for a new statehouse, so the government traded more than three million acres in the panhandle to a group of investors in exchange for their financing of the capitol. The ranch that resulted, the legendary XIT, stretched from north to south more than 200 miles.

This drive begins in Lubbock and heads north to Amarillo and beyond. Along the way, visit the edge of the Cap Rock Escarpment, the dramatic and geologically fascinating boundary between the High Plains and the Rolling Plains to the east.

❶ **Lubbock** *(Convention & Tourism Bureau, 14th St. and Ave. K. 800-692-4035)* grew up as a ranching and farming center on Yellow House Draw, one of the few streams in the south plains region. Fans of Buddy Holly gather each September for an annual tribute to the legendary rock and roller who was born here in 1936; the city has

Ranching Heritage Center of the Museum of Texas Tech University, Lubbock

erected a **Buddy Holly statue** *(8th St. and Ave. Q)* down-town, where he stands in perpetuity holding his Fender Stratocaster guitar. Check with the Tourism Bureau for a guide to other Holly sites, including his first home and the grave where he was buried after a fatal plane crash in 1959.

Today, Lubbock is a lively city centered on Texas Tech University, home of the **Museum of Texas Tech University** *(4th St. and Indiana Ave. 806-742-2490. Closed Mon.)* and, just next door, the excellent **Ranching Heritage Center of the Museum of Texas Tech University**★ *(806-742-2482. Closed Mon.).* The museum offers a collection of pre-Columbian jewelry, pottery, and other artifacts, along with galleries of southwestern art and photogravures by Edward Curtis, who chronicled the lives of Native Americans in the early 1900s.

The Ranching Heritage Center has gathered 35 historic buildings from around Texas, all nicely restored and displayed on a 14-acre site. The structures range from log cabins and a primitive half-dugout to a 1909 Queen Anne-style house built by a prosperous rancher in nearby Hale County. Among them are buildings from such famed Texas ranches as the XIT, the JA Ranch of Charles Goodnight and John Adair, and the King Ranch in southern Texas. Cattle pens, windmills, a cotton gin, a school-house, and a 1918 Santa Fe depot are part of the exhibit, which rewards the visitor with a better understanding of life on the prairies in pioneer times.

To travel further back in time, drive north a short distance to **Lubbock Lake Landmark State Historical Site**

Buddy Holly statue

Palo Duro Canyon State Park

(2401 Landmark Dr. 806-765-0737. Closed Mon.; adm. fee). In 1936 two boys out exploring the Farmers' Reservoir, built in the ancient Yellow House Draw, discovered bones and artifacts—archaeological examinations soon revealed evidence of constant human occupation in the area for 12,000 years. Well-designed exhibits in the park museum display bones from some of the ancient animals drawn to the permanent water source here, including camels, giant bison, giant armadillos, and short-faced bears. The animals in turn attracted prehistoric hunters, who left projectile points, drills, scrapers, and other artifacts. Trails lead through areas where discoveries were made, and where archaeologists are still conducting important research.

Head north on I-27 to Plainview and the **Museum of the Llano Estacado** *(1900 W. 8th St. 806-296-4735. Closed Sat.-Sun. Dec.-Feb.),* a small but interesting museum focusing on regional history. The star attraction is the skull of the "Easter elephant," an imperial mammoth found at the nearby town of Easter; the huge beast roamed the plains more than 11,000 years ago, when the climate was cooler and wetter. Museum exhibits also include a full-size model of a Plains Indian campsite, displays on Llano

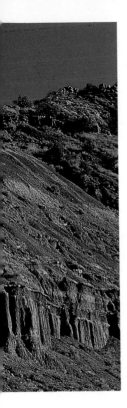

Estacado geology, and a mini-Main Street of a frontier town.

Follow Tex. 194 and US 385 northwest to Hereford for another noteworthy small museum. The **Deaf Smith County Museum** *(400 Sampson St. 806-363-7070. Closed Sun.)* takes as its theme the life of turn-of-the-century pioneers in this county named for Erastus "Deaf" Smith, a scout for Sam Houston in the Texas war of independence. Period household furnishings, farm implements, railroad memorabilia, supplies from an old-time general store, and Indian artifacts fill the rooms of a 1927 schoolhouse.

Turn south off US 60 onto Rte. 168 to reach ❷ **Buffalo Lake National Wildlife Refuge** *(806-499-3382. Adm. fee)*, a 7,600-acre preserve of prairie, marsh, and cropland. The lake that once hosted masses of wintering waterfowl has long been mostly dry, but the refuge is still a good place to see wildlife, including coyotes, mule deer, and badgers. The 0.5-mile **Cottonwood Canyon Trail** is a pleasant walk beside a low cliff, where a variety of songbirds flit through the trees and shrubs. Don't miss a visit to the prairie-dog town east of Rte. 168, where you can stand quietly and watch these funny little creatures at play. Prairie dogs (which are not dogs but rodents) once populated the plains in the untold millions, but persecution and land development have drastically lowered their numbers.

Continue east on US 60 to Canyon, where you'll find one of Texas' finest museums and the panhandle's single most rewarding attraction: the **Panhandle-Plains Historical Museum** ★ ★ *(2401 4th Ave. 806-656-2244. Donation)*, on the campus of West Texas A&M University. The expansive halls here house displays on geology, paleontology, ranching, the oil business, wildlife, and Plains Indians, to list some of the highlights. The museum's Pioneer Town is far more extensive than most similar exhibits, re-creating an early panhandle settlement with a bank, saloon, print shop, general store, livery stable, and many other buildings, including a log cabin built about 1881 by famed cattleman Charles Goodnight and

Caprock Canyons

One of Texas' most beautiful natural areas is **Caprock Canyons State Park** *(Rte. 1065. 806-455-1492. Adm. fee)*, located just north of the small town of Quitaque, east of Tulia. Like Palo Duro Canyon State Park to the northwest, Caprock lies on the edge of the escarpment for which the park is named, where small streams have eroded deep ravines and spectacular rock formations in the tall bluff that separates the High Plains from the lower Rolling Plains. Caprock sees far fewer visitors than Palo Duro, though, and so offers greater opportunity for solitary exploration of the rugged badlands along its backcountry trails. Mesquite, sage, juniper, and cactus grow in the park's drier areas, while cottonwood, plum, and hackberry can be found in the canyon's bottoms. The park also is home to mule deer, badgers, porcupines, and Charles Goodnight's JA herd of bison.

19

used as a line camp on his ranch in Palo Duro Canyon.

Elsewhere in the museum you'll find a diorama of a mastodon and tiny horses that lived in the area more than five million years ago, and the skeleton of a ground sloth the size of a modern-day horse. There's a fine display of antique cars, buggies, and wagons; an extensive collection of weapons; an entire wing of petroleum-related exhibits; and a room full of historic windmills, so important to the development of the plains. If you stop here an hour before closing, don't expect to be able to take it all in.

Follow Tex. 217 east to beautiful **Palo Duro Canyon State Park** ★ *(806-488-2227. Adm. fee)*, a landscape in striking contrast to the flat plains you've been traversing. Palo Duro sits on the Cap Rock Escarpment, the eastern boundary of the Llano Estacado. Here the harder rock that lies just under the surface is slowly eroding away, exposing the softer sandstone, shale, mudstone, and gypsum underneath and creating a spectacle often compared, quite aptly, to a smaller-scale Grand Canyon. Over the past million years or so, the Prairie Dog Town Fork Red River has cut down nearly 800 feet through the cliffs, exposing brightly colored layers of rock sculptured in weird and wonderful ways. Although the panoramas from the park road are splendid, you should make time to hike the 4.5-mile round-trip **Lighthouse Trail** for a close-up look at this geological marvel.

❸ Amarillo *(Visitor Council 806-374-1497 or 800-692-1338)* takes its name from the Spanish word for yellow; the first settlement here, originally a collection of railroad workers' tents, was named for a nearby creek, which itself was named for the locality's yellowish earth. Today's city is the crossroads and economic center of the Texas Panhandle, known for ranching and, uniquely, for producing

90 percent of the world's helium. That distinction is noted by a skeletal-looking Helium Monument on the grounds of the **Don Harrington Discovery Center** *(1200 Streit Dr. 806-355-9547. Closed Mon.; adm. fee for special shows and planetarium)*, a science technology center and

---

Auto Art?

Fans of things peculiar should drive west of Amarillo on I-40 a few miles to **Cadillac Ranch** *(Helium Rd. exit)*, where in 1974 an eccentric local businessman, in collaboration with a group of artists from San Francisco, planted ten luxury cars grille-first in a field. You're welcome to walk out among the cars and take photos, or even to write your name or a special message on a fender. What you'll see is no more and no less than described: ten rusty, graffiti-marked Cadillacs partially buried in a field. The scene, undoubtedly Amarillo's most famous, occupies its own unique place somewhere in that gray area between conceptual art and a crazy whim.

20

Cadillac Ranch, near Amarillo

planetarium named for a local oilman and philanthropist. Though the center's interactive exhibits are aimed primarily at kids, adults will have a hard time resisting the chance to make a tornado or play with experiments in physics and optics.

Horse lovers will enjoy the **American Quarter Horse Heritage Center and Museum** *(Quarter Horse Dr., off I-40. 806-376-5181. Closed Sun.-Mon. Labor Day–April; adm. fee)*, devoted to the popular mount named for its speed in quarter-mile races. Displays begin with a look at prehistoric horses such as the fox-size *Eohippus,* tracing the development of the quarter horse through the days of match races and cattle drives to the modern breed.

Exploring at the Don Harrington Discovery Center

As early as 12,000 years ago, Paleo-Indians discovered a rich source of colorful flint near what is now called the Canadian River, north of Amarillo. They used sticks or bone tools to extract the material, which they then shaped into dart points, arrowheads, knives, and other objects. Use of the quarries here continued for thousands of years; the flint, a valued trade item, has been found all across the plains and Southwest, hundreds of miles from its origin.

This important ancient resource is preserved as ❹ **Alibates Flint Quarries National Monument** *(Tex. 136, S of Fritch. 806-857-3151)*, on the slopes south of Lake Meredith, on the now-dammed Canadian River. Admission to the site is by ranger-led tours only; tours are given twice daily from Memorial Day to Labor Day, and by reservation only the remainder of the year. Visitors see excavations made by Indian diggers, as well as abundant chunks of multicolored flint discarded in the mining process.

At Borger, take Tex. 207 south to the town of Panhandle and the **Square House Museum** *(5th and Elsie Sts. 806-537-3524)*, a complex of several structures interpreting the history of Carson County and the panhandle. The central feature is the Square House itself, a small frame residence built in the 1880s with lumber transported by oxcart from Dodge City, Kansas; the city's oldest structure, it's full of local memorabilia, such as a pair of wooden shoes brought to America by a German immigrant and worn by his son as he walked behind a plow. Elsewhere on the grounds stands a 1928 Santa Fe caboose, a windmill, and a reconstruction of a half-dugout home of the type used by pioneer families on the plains before the turn of the century, furnished with a trundle bed, pie safe, and potbellied stove that kept the interior cozy by burning cow chips.

● **675 miles** ● **5 to 7 days** ● **Fall through spring**
● Distances between towns and services can be great in West Texas; be sure your car is in good condition and check fuel often. ● Accommodations are very limited in and around Big Bend National Park; make reservations in advance.

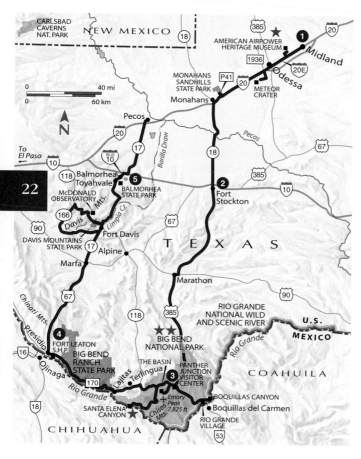

At the heart of this Texas-size drive lies one of the world's great wild places: Big Bend National Park, an immense preserve of stark desert and rugged mountains, bounded by canyons carved hundreds of feet deep by the relentless flow of the Rio Grande. To the north of the park rise the Davis Mountains—not as spectacular as Big Bend (very little is), but well worth visiting for their own striking landscape; in addition, they're home to a restored Old West fort and the famed McDonald Observatory.

The route begins in the oil city of Midland and heads west to the peculiar expanse of the Monahans Sandhills before turning south to Big Bend, on the Mexican border. Then it's back north through Fort Davis to finish in the little town of Pecos. Along the way you'll see some fine museums, noteworthy historic sites, and more wide-open space than you ever knew existed.

As I-20 spans the long, long stretch between Dallas and the Davis Mountains, it bisects the area of West Texas known as the Permian Basin—a region covered by a shallow sea more than 200 million years ago, known now for rich oil deposits. (The bobbing heads of pumping units are a ubiquitous part of the scene in these parts.) The twin "capitals" of the basin are the adjacent cities of **① Midland** *(Chamber of Commerce 915-683-3381 or 800-624-6435)* and **Odessa** *(Chamber of Commerce 915-333-7871 or 800-780-4678)*—both of which have seen their fortunes rise and fall with the price of crude since oil was discovered here in 1920. Midland's **Permian Basin Petroleum Museum★** *(1500 I-20 W. 915-683-4403. Adm. fee)* deals not just with the oil business but with regional history all the way back to that Permian-period sea, in a realistic diorama depicting some of the creatures that inhabited ancient ocean reefs. The museum also includes the world's largest collection of antique oil-drilling equipment, a re-creation of an old-time oil boomtown, and displays on modern-day oil production.

At the Midland International Airport, the **American Airpower Heritage Museum★** *(9600 Wright Dr. 915-563-1000. Adm. fee)* centers on a collection of World War II aviation artifacts that tell the story of the Confederate Air Force, an organization devoted to preserving vintage airplanes. Located in the main hangar are planes on rotating display from the CAF's 140-plane collection. A special museum exhibit details the military career of President George Bush, whose torpedo bomber was shot down in the South Pacific in September 1944. In a separate museum building, exhibits trace the course of airpower, from the Spanish Civil War through the dropping of atomic bombs on Japan.

Monahans Sandhills State Park

George Bush lived in the Midland-Odessa area in the 1950s, when he was getting his start in the oil business; he, of course, is among the chief executives featured at Odessa's **Presidential Museum** *(622 N. Lee Ave. 915-332-7123. Tues.-Sat.; adm. fee),* full of memorabilia from past elections—posters, pins, and political cartoons—as well as miniatures of the First Ladies' inaugural gowns. For a look a bit further back in history, take a walk around Odessa's **meteor crater** *(Rte. 1936 exit off I-20 and follow signs),* a 500-foot-wide shallow depression among the mesquite trees and oil wells west of town, where an

Annie Riggs Memorial Museum, Fort Stockton

iron-nickel meteor struck the earth 20,000 years ago.

Continue west on I-20 to **Monahans Sandhills State Park** *(Park Rd. 41. 915-943-2092. Adm. fee),* which encompasses part of an extensive field of dunes stretching north into New Mexico. This huge volume of sand, once lying along ancient riverbeds, was picked up by prevailing winds and deposited here in a dry period after the last ice age. The park road leads to an area of very tall dunes; kids may enjoy renting a plastic disk and "surfing" down the slopes.

Turn south on Tex. 18 to ❷ **Fort Stockton** *(Tourism Information Center 915-336-8052),* which began in 1858 as an Army camp. A more permanent post was established in 1867, and endures today at **Historic Fort Stockton** *(Rooney and 3rd Sts. 915-336-2400. June–Labor Day daily, closed Sun. rest of year; adm. fee),* a combination of original and reconstructed buildings that re-create part of the 19th-century frontier outpost. Exhibits include clothing, weapons, and a scale model of the original Fort Stockton.

Not far away, the **Annie Riggs Memorial Museum** *(301 S. Main. 915-336-2167. Adm. fee)* is housed in a 1900 adobe hotel that once accommodated passengers on the Butterfield stage line. Named for the woman who first managed, then owned the hotel, the museum includes in its varied collection a desk at which a local sheriff was killed in 1894, an original hotel bed (bought from Sears,

Rio Grande winding through Canyon Colorado, Big Bend Ranch State Park

Roebuck in 1900 for $6.75), and a set of Annie Riggs's rules for guests (one example: "All boisterous and profane language strictly forbidden").

Prepare now for a long drive across a very lonely landscape—but at the end waits a splendid reward. Ninety-eight miles down US 385 sprawls **Big Bend National Park**★ ★ *(915-477-2251. Adm. fee)*, truly a gem among America's parks. Stretching across 801,163 acres along the Rio Grande, Big Bend offers the traveler an endless list of rewards, from mountain vistas to the tiny Colima warbler, a bird that nests here and nowhere else in the United States.

The greater part of the park landscape is Chihuahuan Desert, a distinctive ecosystem that, though seemingly arid and barren, can burst into colorful bloom after a wet spring season. In the center of Big Bend rise the magnificent Chisos Mountains, reaching their zenith at 7,825-foot Emory Peak; with a higher rainfall level than the surrounding desert, the park highlands are home to trees such as Douglas-fir, drooping juniper, and Texas madrone, as well as mountain lion and a localized race of white-tailed deer.

Make your first stop the ❸ **Panther Junction Visitor Center;** here you can look over a selection of maps and guidebooks and walk a short nature trail that introduces some of the desert plants, including the spectacular century plant, an agave that sends its flowering stalk shooting upwards to 15 feet or more. Then drive east to **Rio Grande Village,** where there's another interesting nature walk and, nearby, a short trail into **Boquillas Canyon.**

Return to Panther Junction and continue west to the turnoff leading up to the **Basin.** Here in the heart of the Chisos Mountains you'll find a lodge, restaurant, campground, and trailheads for hikes ranging from easy strolls to high-country backpacking trips. The energetic hike up the Pinnacles Trail, through Boot Canyon, and back down the Laguna Meadow Trail offers fabulous scenery.

In the park's southwestern corner, **Santa Elena Canyon**★ ranks with Big Bend's most wondrous sights. Here, the erosive power of the Rio Grande has sliced through hundreds of feet of rock, sculpturing chasms with sheer cliffs towering above the narrow ribbon of water at their base. A short trail leads into the canyon; park visitor centers can provide information on outfitters for rafting trips through Santa Elena and other Big Bend canyons.

On Rte. 170 just west of the park, **Terlingua** survives mostly as a ghost town, with a few ruined buildings remaining from its days as a center of mercury mining. In November, though, the Terlingua area briefly comes to life when it hosts a famed chili-cooking competition

Mighty Flier

Fossils of several types of dinosaurs and other ancient creatures have been found in the Big Bend area, including duck-billed dinosaurs and a crocodile estimated to have been 50 feet long. The most amazing, however, is the giant pterodactyl, named *Quetzalcoatlus northropi*, found in Big Bend National Park in 1971. With a wingspan estimated at 36 to 39 feet, it was the largest flying creature ever to exist on earth. The original fossil wing bones are displayed at the University of Texas Memorial Museum in Austin (see p. 47); Houston's Museum of Natural Science (see p. 54) has a full-size model of *Quetzalcoatlus*'s entire skeleton looming over its dinosaur room, giving a hint of the incredible spectacle this monster must have presented as it soared through the skies of what is now West Texas.

(information 915-772-2379), featuring hundreds of chefs and an enthusiastic following of fans.

The 50 miles of Rte. 170 between Lajitas and Presidio, known as **El Camino del Rio** (the River Road), constitute one of Texas' finest scenic drives. The highway follows the Rio Grande, constantly twisting and turning, climbing and descending, always providing superb views of rugged terrain. Along the way, you'll pass through **Big Bend Ranch State Park** *(915-229-3416. Adm. fee)*, a vast primitive area protecting nearly 290,000 acres of Chihuahuan Desert. The park's **Barton Warnock Environmental Education Center** *(915-424-3327. Adm. fee)* at Lajitas is a good place to learn about the region, with exhibits on desert ecology and an interpretive garden. Hiking trails lead to backcountry areas; call the park office for information on guided bus tours.

East of Presidio, **❹ Fort Leaton State Historical Park** *(Rte. 170. 915-229-3416. Adm. fee)* stands as an evocative memento of frontier days on the Rio Grande. Begun in 1848 as a home, business headquarters, and private fortress by rancher-trader Benjamin Leaton, the partially restored adobe fort comprises more than 25 rooms surrounding a courtyard. Exhibits recount the area's colorful history, from Native Americans to Ben Leaton's notorious beginnings as a scalp hunter to the fort's service as headquarters for a troop of Texas Rangers.

At Presidio, take US 67 north through the Chinati Mountains to Marfa (see sidebar this page); continuing north on Tex. 17 brings you to nearly mile-high **Fort Davis** *(Chamber of Commerce 915-426-3015 or 800-524-3015)*. On the outskirts of town, **Fort Davis National Historic Site** *(Tex. 17. 915-426-3224. Adm. fee)* is the best preserved of the many 19th-century military posts built to protect travelers and mail shipments on pioneer trails in the Southwest. Although the fort was established in 1854, the present configuration dates from 1867. Restored stone-and-adobe buildings include officers' quarters, barracks, and the post hospital.

An Army officer passing through the West Texas area in 1856 wrote that, while much of the region was harsh desert, "there are, however, oases of surpassing beauty…" You'll find just such a place at nearby **Davis Mountains State Park** *(Tex. 118. 915-426-3337. Adm. fee)*. Oak, juniper, and sumac dot the slopes, providing habitat for rock squirrels, mule deer, and the elusive Montezuma quail. The park has a scenic drive to a mountain ridgetop, campsites, and the **Indian Lodge** *(915-426-3254)*, a Pueblo-style inn.

Tex. 118 is known as the highest paved road east of the Rocky Mountains; following it west from the park

Marfa Lights

Though it gained a bit of celebrity when James Dean, Elizabeth Taylor, and Rock Hudson came to town to film the 1955 movie *Giant*, the hamlet of Marfa is best known for the Marfa lights, a phenomenon that's partly a genuine mystery and partly a well-promoted tourist attraction. For well over a century people have been seeing strange, inexplicable lights moving above the desert east of town; theories on their source include glowing rocks, swamp gas, ghosts, secret military experiments, and luminous jackrabbits. If you'd like to look for yourself, there's an official viewing area on US 90 nine miles east of town.

26

leads to the University of Texas' **McDonald Observatory** *(915-426-3640. Fee for tours),* sitting atop Mount Locke at an elevation of nearly 6,800 feet. One of the world's most important astronomical research institutions, the observatory offers

Fort Davis National Historic Site

daily solar viewing and three-times-weekly star parties. Check for guided tours of the new 430-inch Hobby-Eberly optical telescope, second largest on earth.

Continuing northwest on Tex. 118 and turning south on Tex. 166 will take you on a 74-mile loop back to Fort Davis. This drive winding through the rolling terrain of the Davis Mountains is one of the state's most renowned scenic routes, with excellent wildlife viewing opportunities for species ranging from golden eagles and songbirds to coyotes and pronghorn.

North on Tex. 17 in Toyahvale, ❺ **Balmorhea State Park** *(Tex. 17. 915-375-2370. Adm. fee)* is noted as the site of San Solomon Springs, which supply a swimming pool covering 1.75 acres and holding 3.5 million gallons of water. Several species of fish live in the pool, including the endangered Comanche Springs pupfish; the water's excellent visibility makes for fine snorkeling and diving. The park has re-created a portion of the original naturally occurring desert wetland, to demonstrate what the spring environment was like before man's alterations.

The best thing about the **West of the Pecos Museum** *(1st and Cedar Sts. 915-445-5076. Closed Sun.; adm. fee)* in Pecos is the building itself—or rather, buildings. One section is a former saloon constructed by an ex-Texas Ranger in 1896; an adjacent three-story hotel, built eight years later, continued in operation until the 1950s. The hotel's rooms now display a range of local historical items, including Indian artifacts, antiques, and rodeo memorabilia. The saloon boasts an attraction you won't find in just any museum: Plaques in the floor mark the spots where two men fell, shot in a brief but deadly gunfight in 1896.

If time permits further exploration of West Texas, follow I-20 and I-10 200 miles to El Paso for the El Paso-Guadalupe Excursion (see pages 28-29).

● **200 miles from Pecos** ● **110-mile excursion**

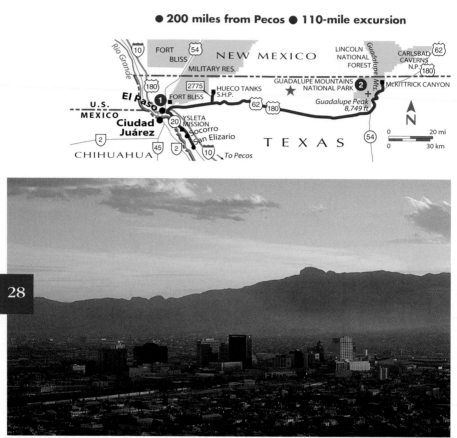

El Paso at sunset

28

In May 1598 Spanish conquistador Don Juan de Oñate led a colonizing expedition across the Rio Grande, which he called *el paso del rio del norte,* the pass of the river of the north. That crossing spot became today's city of ❶ **El Paso** *(Convention & Visitors Bureau 915-534-0696 or 800-351-6024),* at the western tip of Texas on the Rio Grande. The Spanish founded missions in the area in the 17th and 18th centuries; although all have been rebuilt after floods and fire, three churches established in that era endure as notable historic sites: the chapel of **San Elizario** *(Socorro Rd., San Elizario. 915-851-2333),* **Socorro Mission** *(328 S. Nevarez Rd., Socorro. 915-859-7718. Mon.-Fri.),* and **Ysleta Mission** *(131 S. Zaragosa Rd. 915-859-9848).* You can learn about El Paso's colorful history—which encompasses Indian wars, Old West outlaw John Wesley Hardin, and Pancho Villa—at two museums: the **El Paso Museum of History** *(12901 Gateway W. Blvd. 915-858-1928. Mon.-Sat.)* and the **University of Texas at El Paso's Centennial**

Museum *(University Ave. and Wiggins Rd. 915-747-5565. Tues.-Sat.).* Downtown, **Magoffin Home State Historical Park** *(1120 Magoffin Ave. 915-533-5147. Wed.-Sun.; adm. fee)* centers on a house built in 1875 by one of the area's pioneer settlers. The 19-room residence, with 3-foot-thick walls of adobe brick, exemplifies a style of architecture known as Southwest Territorial; it still contains many furnishings and personal items of the Magoffin family.

The city is also home to the U.S. Army's Fort Bliss, established in 1849 and moved several times before settling in its current location. The fort's early days are recalled at the **Fort Bliss Museum** *(Pleasanton Rd. and Sheridan Dr. 915-568-4518),* located in an adobe building recreating the post's appearance in the 1850s; the nearby **U.S. Army Air Defense Artillery Museum** *(Bldg. 5000, Pleasanton Rd. 915-568-5412)* focuses on the history of air defense since 1917.

The permanent water supplies found at **Hueco Tanks State Historical Park** *(Rte. 2775. 915-857-1135. Adm. fee),* east of El Paso, have attracted human visitors for perhaps 12,000 years; Indians from many different eras left 3,000 pictographs on the rugged rocks that rise up abruptly here like islands in the desert. The site also served as a stop on the Butterfield stage line in the late 19th century, and ruins of the old station can still be seen. In addition to the park's historical interest, it's an excellent place to observe wildlife, concentrated here by the oasis effect of permanent water in an arid landscape.

Farther east, ❷ **Guadalupe Mountains National Park**★ *(Off US 62/180. 915-828-3251. No facilities)* constitutes one of Texas' premier natural areas. Among its attractions, the park includes the state's highest point: 8,749-foot Guadalupe Peak. As astounding as it seems, these massive mountains are actually part of a reef system that grew in a tropical ocean about 250 million years ago.

29

Hikers in McKittrick Canyon, Guadalupe Mountains National Park

Hiking trails meander throughout the park, including strenuous routes to the top of Guadalupe Peak and into the forested Bowl; an easier trail leads up beautiful McKittrick Canyon, where oaks, maples, walnuts, junipers, and ponderosa pines grow. Plant and animal life in the park are comparable to areas in the Rocky Mountains farther north. Here you'll find the only chipmunks and red squirrels in Texas, as well as Douglas-fir, aspen, elk, mule deer, rainbow trout, and such highland birds as mountain chickadee and band-tailed pigeon.

● **380 miles** ● **3 to 5 days** ● **Year-round** ● **Mid-summer temperatures can be sweltering in the lower Rio Grande Valley, though nearby Gulf beaches offer relief.** ● **Spring-break weeks are a madhouse on South Padre Island; unless you're a college student, you might want to pick another time to visit.**

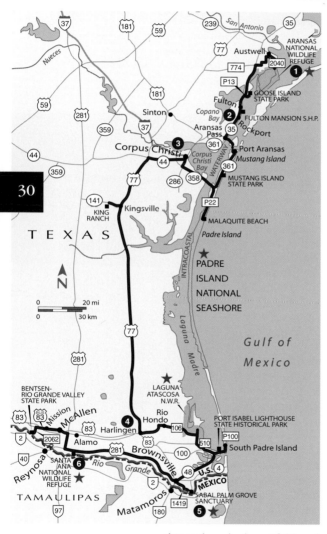

Who's most attracted to the long sweep of Texas' lower Gulf Coast and the Rio Grande Valley? It's not the annual immigrants known as "winter Texans" or "snowbirds," though they come by the thousands in their RVs to escape the northern snows. It's not party-hearty collegians, though they love the beaches and nightlife of South Padre Island. And it's not family vacationers, though there's a lot to do here, from a great aquarium to an equally great zoo to vintage aircraft. Most of all, it's birdwatchers who revere this region. South Texas is home to some of the country's rarest species, as well as plentiful and accessible places to see them. Every serious birder comes to visit eventually, and most return again and again.

But even if you're not part of the binocular-toting crowd, you'll enjoy many of the same things they do: beautiful beaches, fascinating parks and wildlife refuges, the confluence of ocean and subtropical vegetation, and a warm winter climate. South Texas offers diverse—and in many cases unique—attractions in a relatively small area, with the additional appeal of a lively and colorful Hispanic influence in the Rio Grande Valley.

This drive begins at one of the country's most famous wildlife refuges, heading south to Corpus Christi and the unspoiled beaches of Padre Island National Seashore. From there you'll visit the enormous King Ranch en route to the lower Rio Grande Valley, gateway to South Padre Island and a place where you're never far from a good chile relleno.

❶ Aransas National Wildlife Refuge ★ *(Off Rte. 2040, S of Austwell. 512-286-3559. Adm. fee)* offers visitors a long list of wildlife to keep an eye out for, ranging from songbirds and armadillos to hawks, bobcats, javelina, and alligators. The refuge is best known, however, as the only wintering ground of the very rare migrating whooping crane, a species that seemed certain to suffer extinction earlier in this century but that, with strict protection, has made a reasonable comeback. The tall white birds are sometimes spotted from the refuge viewing tower, but a

Whooping crane taking off at Aransas National Wildlife Refuge

better way to see them is to take one of the commercial boat tours leaving from nearby Rockport (see p. 32). Aransas' 16-mile driving route is likely to turn up an excellent variety of birds, mammals, and reptiles.

Take Rte. 774 and Tex. 35 south toward Copano Bay, turning off before the bridge to reach **Goose Island State Park** *(Park Rd. 13. 512-729-2858. Adm. fee),* a small park worth visiting for a look at the "Big Tree," a magnificent live oak estimated to be a thousand years old. With a circumference of 34 feet and a crown spread of 89 feet, a better name for it might be the "Enormous Tree."

On the Trail of Great Birds

Recognizing the popularity of its Gulf Coast region among birdwatchers, Texas has officially established the **Great Texas Coastal Birding Trail**, a driving route that eventually will link more than 300 sites from the Sabine River in the east down to the Rio Grande Valley. Included will be such famous spots as Santa Ana National Wildlife Refuge, near McAllen, and Padre Island National Seashore, near Corpus Christi, as well as lesser-known sites like the Copano Bay State Fishing Pier and the Port Aransas Birding Center, adjoining a wastewater treatment plant. (If that last one seems strange, you should know that birders consider sewer plants excellent places to see migrating shorebirds.) Sites are marked with official highway signs showing a black skimmer, a ternlike seabird. The central part of the trail is already complete, while work on other sections continues; for information write Texas Parks and Wildlife Department, 4200 Smith School Road, Austin, TX 78744.

Across the bay bridge, **Fulton Mansion State Historical Park** *(Fulton Beach Rd. and Henderson St. 512-729-0386. Wed.-Sun.; adm. fee)* centers on an imposing house completed in 1877 by George Fulton, a rancher, engineer, and businessman. The interest of Fulton and his wife, Harriet, in up-to-date conveniences led them to equip the French Second Empire-style mansion with a central ventilation and heating system, gas lighting, flush toilets, and food-cooling troughs. Hourly tours take visitors through the restored interior, furnished with period items.

❷ **Rockport** *(Chamber of Commerce, 404 Broadway. 512-729-6445 or 800-826-6441)* is known for fishing (speckled trout, red drum, black drum, flounder, and sheepshead are favored species) and birding; the Chamber of Commerce offers a birding guidebook to the region and provides information about boat tours to see wintering whooping cranes. The **Texas Maritime Museum** *(1202 Navigation Cir. 512-729-6644. Closed Mon.; adm. fee),* located near the shrimp boats of Rockport Harbor, looks at how the sea, ships, and seagoers have influenced Texas history. A hands-on area for children is designed to resemble a ship's bridge, while historical exhibits span the years from Spanish explorers to modern commercial fishing.

At Aransas Pass, take Tex. 361 across the Intracoastal Waterway (on the ferry, watch for bottle-nosed dolphins as you cross) to **Mustang Island State Park** *(512-749-5246. Adm. fee),* on one of the string of barrier islands that parallel the Texas coast from Mexico north to Galveston. Five miles of beach here invite swimming, sunbathing, fishing, and camping. Farther south, **Padre Island National Seashore** ★ *(512-949-8068. Adm. fee)* encompasses a grand expanse of wild beach and dunes, one of America's longest stretches of undeveloped shoreline. Stop at the Malaquite Beach Visitor Center for an introduction to barrier island ecology and advice on exploring the park. Passenger cars can drive along South Beach for 5 miles from the Visitor Center; beyond that point, four-wheel drive is recommended.

Across Laguna Madre, ❸ **Corpus Christi** *(Convention & Visitors Bureau 512-881-1888 or 800-678-6232)* hugs a bay named by Spanish explorer Alvarez de Piñeda, who entered it on June 24, 1519, the day of the Feast of Corpus Christi. You'll find several of the city's top attractions on the bay front just off US 181, near the port that ranks as the sixth largest in the U.S. in terms of tonnage. At the top of the list is the superb **Texas State Aquarium** ★ *(2710 N. Shoreline Blvd. 800-477-4853. Adm. fee),* which brings the Gulf of Mexico indoors for a close-up look.

Featured habitats include estuaries, marshes, barrier islands, coral reefs, and the popular "Islands of Steel" exhibit illustrating the life around an offshore oil and gas platform. Sharks, skates, seabirds, otters, turtles, and moray eels are among the colorful creatures found in the various displays.

Just next door, the **USS *Lexington*** *(2914 N. Shoreline Blvd. 512-888-4873 or 800-523-9539. Adm. fee)* lets visitors tour one of the most famous aircraft carriers of World War II. The *Lady Lex,* a 910-foot-long carrier commissioned in 1943, was the first carrier to enter Tokyo Bay after the signing of the peace treaty with Japan. Several tour routes wind through the huge ship, providing looks at officers' and crew quarters, sick bay, the engine room, and the bridge. Restored aircraft on the flight deck include a WWII-era Avenger torpedo bomber and an F-14 Navy jet.

You can see ships of a very different sort in the Columbus Fleet at the **Corpus Christi Museum of Science and History** *(1900 N. Chaparral St. 512-883-2862. Adm. fee)*. Faithful copies of Christopher Columbus's ships *Niña, Pinta,* and *Santa María,* built by the Spanish government to commemorate the 500th anniversary of the explorer's historic first voyage, are on display here; the contrast between the mammoth *Lexington* and the diminutive early ships is remarkable. A special exhibit in the museum examines the interactions of Native Americans and Europeans after the two cultures came into contact in 1492.

Take US 77 south into **Kingsville** *(Visitors Bureau 512-592-8516 or 800-333-5032),* a town whose history is inextricably tied to that of the celebrated **King Ranch.** Founded by steamboat captain Richard King in 1853, the ranch grew enormously over the decades and now covers

At the Texas State Aquarium, Corpus Christi

825,000 acres in four divisions—a total area a bit larger than the state of Rhode Island. The ranch's Visitor Center *(Tex. 141. 512-592-8055. Fee for tours)* offers tours of part of this empire, including an exterior look at the house built in 1912 by Henrietta King, Richard's widow. In Kingsville, the **King Ranch Museum** *(405 N. 6th St. 512-595-1881. Adm. fee)* features historic photos of ranch life taken by a *Life* magazine photographer in the 1940s, antique cars, saddles, and other memorabilia.

Continuing south on US 77 leads into ❹ **Harlingen** *(Chamber of Commerce 956-423-5440 or 800-531-7346)*, where you've officially arrived in the lower Rio Grande Valley (or simply "the Valley," in Texan shorthand). Get a taste of local history at the **Rio Grande Valley Museum** *(Boxwood and Raintree Sts. 956-430-8500. Wed.-Sun.; donation)*, a complex of five buildings with changing exhibits on varied aspects of Harlingen's past, the Valley, and Texas. The Paso Real Stagecoach Inn, dating from the 1850s, was moved here from its original location on Arroyo Colorado; antique medical equipment, natural history displays, and the restored residence of Lon Hill, Harlingen's founder, are among other museum attractions.

Not far away, the **Texas Iwo Jima Memorial** *(320 Iwo Jima Blvd. 956-412-2207)* is the original full-size model used

AD-5 Sky Raider at the Texas Air Museum

to cast the famous bronze statue depicting the raising of the United States flag on Iwo Jima's Mount Suribachi in World War II. (The bronze version stands near Arlington National Cemetery outside Washington, D.C.) The adjacent Iwo Jima Museum and Gift Shop contains military artifacts and shows a film on the battle for the island.

Follow Rte. 106 east of Rio Hondo to the **Texas Air Museum** *(Rte. 106. 956-748-2112. Adm. fee)*, whose collection of aircraft and artifacts date from an 1913 air encounter with Pancho Villa. Stay on Rte. 106 to the turnoff north to **Laguna Atascosa National Wildlife Refuge** ★ *(956-748-3607. Adm. fee)*, one of several fine natural areas you'll find in the Valley. This 45,000-acre refuge encompasses ponds, marshes, brushland, and shoreline along Laguna Madre, providing habitat for wintering waterfowl, the rare and seldom seen ocelot, and many of the specialty birds of the region, including green jay, great

34

kiskadee, and the pheasant-like plain chachalaca.

Take Rte. 510 and Tex. 100 to **Port Isabel Lighthouse State Historical Park** *(Tex. 100. 956-943-1172. Closed for renovation until late 1998; call for schedule),* a 60-foot-tall landmark built in 1853 and active in guiding ships until 1905. From the lighthouse you can get a good view of the hotels and condominiums lining the inviting beaches of **South Padre Island** *(Visitor Center 956-761-6433 or 800-343-2368),* Texas' hottest sea-and-sun vacation center and yearly spring-break headquarters for thousands of students intent on a good time.

If you're interested in a different kind of wild life, take Tex. 48 to **Brownsville** *(Convention & Visitors Bureau 956-546-3721 or 800-626-2639)* and the renowned **Gladys Porter Zoo**★★ *(500 Ringgold St., off Tex. 48. 956-546-2177. Adm. fee),* a facility much honored for its success in breeding endangered species from around the globe. Jentink's duiker (the world's rarest antelope), Przewalski's wild horse, Philippine crocodile, and Malagasy radiated tortoise are among the unusual species found here, along with more familiar types such as elephants, zebras, giraffes, and a great variety of birds and reptiles.

The **Historic Brownsville Museum** *(641 E. Madison St. 956-548-1313. Closed Sun.; adm. fee),* housed in a 1928 Spanish colonial-style railroad depot, offers exhibits on the city's past, including battles fought nearby during the Mexican-American War and the Civil War. The battle of Palmito Ranch was the last land engagement of the latter conflict; it took place May 13, 1865, more than a month after Lee surrendered to Grant at Appomattox Court House. Near the Brownsville airport, the **Confederate Air Force Museum** *(955 Minnesota St. 956-541-8585. Closed Sun.; adm. fee)* comprises a hangar of restored vintage planes and a collection of military artifacts.

One of the country's best small nature preserves is located 5 miles southeast of Brownsville off Rte. 1419 (Southmost Road). The National Audubon Society's ❺ **Sabal Palm Grove Sanctuary**★ *(956-541-8034. Visitor Center open weekends only in summer, Tues.-Sun. rest of year, trails open daily; adm. fee)* is named for the only species of palm native to south Texas, a once common tree now scarce in the state. A small part of the sanctuary protects a grove of mature palms, a woodland striking in its lush, tropical beauty. Elsewhere, plantings are aimed at reproducing the native vegetation that once predominated in the Valley.

Take US 281 west, paralleling the Rio Grande, to ❻ **Santa Ana National Wildlife Refuge**★ *(S of US 281 near Alamo. 956-787-3079. Fee for tram),* a spot that American birdwatchers hold in the same esteem as art lovers do, for example, New York's Metropolitan Museum of Art. Though small (about 2,000 acres), Santa Ana is home to an amazing number of species, including south Texas specialties and strays from Mexico. Countless birders have seen their first altamira oriole, green jay, olive sparrow, or elusive clay-colored robin here. With 95 percent of the native woodlands in the Valley cleared for agriculture and cities, remaining patches like this refuge act as magnets for wildlife—not just birds but species like the giant toad, the beautiful Texas indigo snake, and a long list of butterflies. Trails are open every day, but private vehicles have only limited access to refuge roads in winter, when a passenger tram operates; call for details.

In nearby McAllen, the **McAllen International Museum** *(1900 Nolana St. 956-682-1564. Closed Mon.; adm. fee)* is best known for its collection of Latin American folk art, including masks, pottery, baskets, and textiles, some of which date back to the 17th century. Other areas focus on geology, science, and fine arts.

Finally, just west of Mission, **Bentsen-Rio Grande Valley State Park** *(Rte. 2062. 956-585-1107. Adm. fee)* is another of south Texas' favorite destinations for birders. Roads and trails wind through the park's 587 acres alongside the Rio Grande, offering a chance to see such rarities as hook-billed kite, red-billed pigeon, and green kingfisher. Many of the "winter Texans" in the campground keep feeders well stocked, and it's become a ritual for visiting birdwatchers to wander among the recreational vehicles and check out what's been attracted to the fruit and seeds.

Laguna Atascosa National Wildlife Refuge

● **360 miles** ● **4 to 5 days** ● **Year-round**

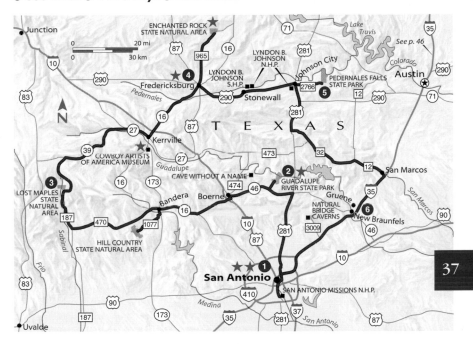

See p. 46

Right smack in the heart of Texas is a place most Texans hold close to their own hearts: the Hill Country. The rolling terrain and rocky rivers you'll find here seem a world apart from the state's sprawling cities—without the lonely emptiness of much of the expanse farther west. It's a land that inspires a relaxed attitude, with plenty of towns catering to travelers, yet with ample opportunities to hike, ride, or paddle through some of the prettiest parks and natural areas in Texas.

On the eastern edge of the Hill Country lies San Antonio, America's ninth largest city, as well as one of its liveliest and most exotic. The proximity of Latin America is manifest here (Hispanics make up more than half the city's population), but salsa is only one ingredient in the cultural smorgasbord you'll sample on this drive. Germans played an early role in settling the area; San Antonio and several nearby cities still reflect their heritage. And travelers who yearn for the Texas of boots, saddles, and Stetson hats will be happy to learn that Bandera, home of several famed dude ranches, calls itself the "Cowboy Capital of the World."

This loop begins in San Antonio and travels west through some of the most rugged parts of the Hill Country before turning northward toward Kerrville, on the

Mission San Antonio de Valero, known as the Alamo

Guadalupe River. It pauses in the distinctly Germanic town of Fredericksburg, makes a short detour to the amazing geological formation called Enchanted Rock, and then heads eastward through the homeland of President Lyndon B. Johnson.

Founded as a Spanish mission in 1718, **❶ San Antonio**★★ *(Convention & Visitors Bureau 210-270-8700 or 800-447-3372)* offers visitors a vibrant downtown scene, colorful history, and a diverse array of museums. All these facets of the city are combined at Mission San Antonio de Valero, far better known as the **Alamo**★ *(300 Alamo Plaza. 210-225-1391).* During the war for Texas independence, 189 known volunteers fought Santa Anna's Mexican army for 13 days here before losing their lives in a final battle on March 6, 1836; Davy Crockett and Jim Bowie were among those who died. Located amid the skyscrapers of downtown San Antonio, this small 1756 church contains Texas patriot memorabilia and exhibits on the battle.

Four other 18th-century Spanish missions comprise **San Antonio Missions National Historical Park** *(210-534-8833),* scattered along several miles of the San Antonio River south of downtown. All of these venerable structures are still active churches. The expansive compound at **Mission San José**★ *(Visitor Center, 6701 San José Dr. 210-932-1001),* with its reconstructed walls and living quarters, provides the best re-creation of 18th-century mission life, as Spanish Franciscan friars brought their beliefs to the local Coahuiltecan Indians.

Among your first stops in San Antonio ought to be the **Tower of the Americas**★ *(600 HemisFair Park. 210-207-8615. Adm. fee),* where an elevator lifts you to an observation platform nearly 600 feet into the air; views encompass the city and extend to the green ridges of the Hill Country to the west. Back on terra firma, walk over to the nearby **Institute of Texan Cultures** *(801 S. Bowie St., in HemisFair Park. 210-458-2300. Closed Mon.; adm. fee),* which showcases the contributions made by more than two dozen ethnic groups to modern Texas society.

By now you may be feeling hungry; if so, it's a good time to see the deservedly famous **Paseo del Rio (River Walk)**★ *(From Auditorium Cir. to King William Historic District),* where all manner of restaurants and shops line the San Antonio River as it flows through the central city, 20 feet below street level. Locals and tourists alike crowd the sidewalks here, eating and shopping, shopping and eating...Hop on a **Yanaguana Cruises boat** *(210-244-5700. Adm. fee)* for an excursion with a guide who'll pass on a bit of local history along the way. Afterwards, climb back up to **La Villita** *(Bet. Villita and E. Nueva Sts. 210-207-8610)*, an arts-and-crafts district adjacent to the River Walk with restored historic buildings dating back to the early 1800s.

A bit farther south, the **King William Historic District** *(King William St. and surrounding area)* was settled by well-to-do Germans in the late 19th century and now includes many refurbished mansions; the San Antonio Conservation Society *(107 King William St. 210-224-6163)* offers a walking tour brochure of the area. The **Steves Homestead Museum** *(509 King William St. 210-225-5924. Adm. fee)*, a three-story Second Empire-style mansion built in 1876, is the district's showplace.

El Mercado, also known as **Market Square** *(Commerce and Santa Rosa Sts. 210-207-8600)*, re-creates the lively, crowded feel of a Mexican marketplace, with vendors offering crafts, food, and folk items; with all the belts and bags on display, the smell of leather is almost intoxicating. The nearby **Spanish Governor's Palace** *(105 Military Plaza. 210-224-0601. Adm. fee)*, built in 1749, was the home of the colonial administrators of Texas; nicely restored and

Along San Antonio's Paseo del Rio, or River Walk

authentically furnished, it conveys a mood of both spareness and elegance.

While you're downtown, don't miss the **Hertzberg Circus Museum** *(210 W. Market St. 210-207-7819. Closed Sun. Sept.-May; adm. fee),* with its big-top memorabilia including a carriage used by the famous midget Tom Thumb, a detailed scale-model tented circus, and old-time posters. It's an amusing twist of history that this lively collection is housed in a dignified 1930s building that was once the San Antonio Public Library.

Along Tex. 16, west of Bandera

Some of San Antonio's best destinations lie north of downtown. Start at the **San Antonio Museum of Art** *(200 W. Jones St. 210-978-8100. Adm. fee),* located in the former Lone Star Brewery, which includes an extensive pre-Columbian collection, Asian art, and a strong showing of ancient Greek and Roman works. The **San Antonio Botanical Gardens** *(555 Funston Pl. 210-207-3250. Adm. fee)* is an eclectic place: Its 33 acres include a large area devoted to native Texas ecosystems; formal rose gardens; a Japanese garden with ponds and waterfalls; and a conservatory complex with ferns, palms, and cactuses. The **Witte Museum** *(3801 Broadway. 210-357-1900. Adm. fee)* focuses on history and science; its well-designed Texas Wild exhibit is an fine introduction to the state's ecological regions.

If you enjoy zoos, you'll love the wonderful **San Antonio Zoo** ★ *(3903 N. St. Mary's St. 210-734-7183. Adm. fee)* in Brackenridge Park, by any standard one of America's best. Plan on a long visit here, admiring creatures from tropical fish to endangered whooping cranes and snow leopards. A little farther north, the **McNay Art Museum** ★ *(6000 N. New Braunfels Ave. 210-824-5368. Closed Mon.; donation)* deserves to be far better known than it is. Housed in a wealthy oil heiress's former mansion, the McNay's collection focuses on the 19th and early 20th centuries, but ranges from Gothic to contemporary; its all-star lineup includes El Greco, Renoir, O'Keeffe, and Hopper, among many others.

Leaving the city behind, head north on US 281 to Tex. 46, then go west a few miles to the turnoff for ❷ **Guadalupe River State Park** ★ *(3350 Park Rd. 31.*

830-438-2656. Adm. fee). Here, typical Hill Country scenery of grassland, oak, and juniper blends with the southeastern-flavored woodland of pecan, sycamore, willow, persimmon, and hackberry. On a summer day, the river's cool water is irresistible—especially after a hike on one of the park trails.

Follow Tex. 46 and Tex. 16 west to **Bandera** *(Visitors Bureau, 1808 Tex. 16. 830-796-3045 or 800-364-3833. Mon.-Sat.),* a town as Western as a well-worn ten-gallon hat. Check with the Visitors Bureau for information on local dude ranches and trail rides; outfitters here specialize in introducing tenderfeet to the cowboy life without making them too saddle sore. While in town, stop by the **Frontier Times Museum** *(510 13th St. 830-796-3864. Adm. fee),* one of those terrifically quirky small-town museums cluttered with things from people's attics, oddities of nature, and just generally browse-worthy stuff. How about a stuffed two-headed goat or a collection of 400 bells and gongs?

By this time you've had a glimpse of the Hill Country; now you'll head into its heart. If you're ready for a little adventure, follow Tex. 173 south to the turnoff for **Hill Country State Natural Area** *(Rte. 1077. 830-796-4413. Thurs.-Mon.; adm. fee),* more than 5,400 acres of mostly undeveloped terrain set aside for hiking, horseback riding, mountain biking, and primitive camping.

Rte. 470 west from Bandera climbs, winds, and descends through a strikingly rugged landscape from the Medina River down to the Sabinal. Here, take Rte. 187 north to yet another lovely park, ❸ **Lost Maples State Natural Area** *(830-966-3413. Adm. fee).* More developed than Hill Country State Natural Area, yet still beautifully unspoiled, this 2,208-acre park was named for its stands of bigtooth maples, which can turn brilliant red-orange in fall. In truth, Lost Maples rewards a visit any time of year, combining scenery, hiking trails, the crystal-clear Sabinal River, and a unique collection of rare, endemic, and unusual plants and animals.

Continue north on Rte. 187 to Tex. 39 and turn eastward, back to the Guadalupe River and **Kerrville** *(Convention & Visitors Bureau 830-792-3535 or 800-221-7958),* long a favorite Texas vacation and weekend-getaway spot. Stop first at the **Hill Country Museum** *(226 Earl Garrett St. 830-896-8633. Closed Sun.; adm. fee),* housed in a stone mansion built in 1879 for Charles Schreiner, a French-born settler who became a successful businessman and a major Hill Country landowner. Schreiner brought in European stonecarvers to work on his home, which boasts fabulous interior woodwork, French chandeliers, and Victorian antiques. Regardless of your taste in art, don't neglect the

Down Under

Millennia of erosion have carved caves throughout the limestone of the Hill Country; you can hardly miss billboards for tours wherever you go. **Natural Bridge Caverns** *(Rte. 3009, NE of San Antonio. 210-651-6101. Adm. fee)* may be the best, with countless extravagantly diverse formations along nearly a mile of trail. Also worth a visit is the small **Cave Without a Name** *(325 Kreutzberg Rd., off Rte. 474, N of Boerne. 210-537-4212. Closed Tues.; adm. fee),* whose unusual non-name derives from a child's entry in a long-ago contest to choose a title for the place: The cave, the boy said, was "too pretty to name."

41

Enchanted Rock State Natural Area

Cowboy Artists of America Museum★ *(1550 Bandera Hwy./Tex. 173. 830-896-2553. Adm. fee)*, which exhibits works by modern artists carrying on the Western tradition of Charles M. Russell and Frederic Remington.

For music lovers within the Lone Star State's borders and well beyond, Kerrville's greatest claim to fame is the annual **Kerrville Folk Festival**★ *(830-257-3600)*, which has grown since its founding in 1972 into an 18-day songwriter festival of eclectic folk-style music. The concerts and accompanying fun begin the Thursday before Memorial Day at Quiet Valley Ranch, 9 miles south of town on Tex. 16; plan well ahead if you want to attend.

Just north on Tex. 16, ❹ **Fredericksburg**★ *(Visitors Bureau 830-997-6523)* was founded in 1846 by German settlers, and today retains a distinctively German feel, modified by a century and a half of Texas influence: sauerbraten roasted over mesquite, say. Old World *Fachwerk* (half-timbered, half-stone) buildings are still in evidence, and you can pick up a German-style pastry at a bakery on Main Street. Learn about the town's past at the **Pioneer Museum Complex** *(309 W. Main St. 830-997-2835. Adm. fee)*, a collection of several historic buildings. At the turn of the century it was a long trip into Fredericksburg for many area farm families, so they often built tiny "Sunday houses" in town for use between Saturday shopping and church; the Weber House on the museum grounds is a good example of this specialized dwelling.

The nearby **Vereins Kirche Museum** *(100 W. Main St. 830-997-7832. Adm. fee)* is a 1935 reconstruction of an 1846 structure that served as a church and meeting hall. Local historical items are featured inside, but the exterior is the most interesting part: One look at the distinctive shape of this octagonal building with its cupola on top and you'll know why it was called *die Kaffee-Muhle-Kirche* (the Coffee Mill Church).

A few blocks east on Main Street stands the excellent **Admiral Nimitz Museum and Historical Center** ★ *(340 E. Main St. 830-997-4379. Adm. fee),* named for Fredericksburg native Chester W. Nimitz, commander in chief of the U.S. Pacific Fleet in World War II. Nimitz's grandfather was one of the town's original settlers; his hotel, begun in 1852 and later much enlarged, has been restored and now houses exhibits on his grandson's military career and the war in the Pacific. An important collection of airplanes, tanks, torpedos, and other weapons is displayed along the **History Walk of the Pacific War,** while the **Japanese Garden of Peace,** a gift from the nation that Nimitz helped defeat, provides a contemplative spot in which to consider the lesssons of that terrible conflict.

Do not leave Fredericksburg without making the short trip north on Rte. 965 to **Enchanted Rock State Natural Area** ★ *(915-247-3903. Adm. fee),* one of the most remarkable sights in the Hill Country, not to say in all of Texas. At the center of this 1,643-acre park is a mammoth dome of pink granite rising more than 400 feet above the surrounding terrain. This billion-year-old geological feature is the second largest granite formation in America, only behind Georgia's Stone Mountain. Even if all you do is look, you'll be glad you came; better still, make the 0.6-mile, steep climb up the **Summit Trail** for a fine panorama of rugged, oak-covered hills.

Back at Fredericksburg, take US 290 east alongside the

Pedernales River, which—as everyone knows who's old enough to remember President Lyndon Johnson's down-home speech—is pronounced Purd'n-AL-iss. At tiny Stonewall you'll find the **Lyndon B. Johnson National Historical Park** *(830-868-7128)* and the adjoining **Lyndon B. Johnson State Historical Park** *(US 290, 2 miles E of Stonewall. 830-644-2252),* both dedicated to the memory of America's 36th President, who was born right here on the river's north bank.

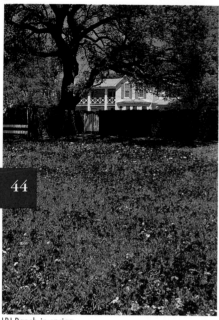

44

LBJ Ranch in spring

National park bus tours *(fee),* which begin at the state park Visitor Center, take visitors through the **LBJ Ranch** and past the one-room school Johnson once attended, a reconstruction of his birthplace, and the family cemetery where he is buried. The state park includes a living history farm that interprets rural Hill Country life in 1918, plus exhibits on Johnson's boyhood and political career.

A half hour to the east lies **Johnson City** (named, of course, for LBJ's pioneer forebears), where another unit of the national park comprises **Johnson's Boyhood Home,** with family possessions and 1920s furnishings, and **Johnson Settlement,** a complex of restored ranch buildings owned by LBJ's grandfather and granduncle from 1867 to 1872.

President Johnson loved the Hill Country and the Pedernales, and during the troubles with Vietnam he often spoke of his homeland fondly, as a place of respite from worries and responsibility. To better understand his feelings, drive 8 miles east from Johnson City on Rte. 2766 to ❺ **Pedernales Falls State Park** *(830-868-7304. Adm. fee),* bordering 6 miles of the river in an area of outstanding scenic beauty. The falls show 300-million-year-old limestone strata that were tilted by the Llano Uplift, a geological event that saw a huge mass of molten rock surge upward toward, but not quite to, the surface. Swimming and tubing aren't allowed at the falls, but are permitted at points farther downstream. Among the park's fine hiking trails, the .25-mile **Hill Country Nature Trail** provides a good introduction to some of the flora and fauna found here. For a tougher challenge, hike or bike the 8-mile **Wolf Mountain Trail,** along which you may see an armadillo, a white-tailed deer, or a coyote—but no wolves.

Return to Johnson City and take US 281 south to Rte. 32, one of the Hill Country's most famous drives: The next 24 miles east have been nicknamed the **"Devil's**

Backbone" for the way the road winds along an exposed ridgetop. At Rte. 12, continue eastward to **San Marcos** *(Chamber of Commerce 512-393-5900).* The San Marcos River rises from the earth here at springs producing more than 150 million gallons of water each day. The river's source is a well-publicized commercial attraction called **Aquarena Center** *(One Aquarena Springs Dr. 512-245-7575 or 800-999-9767);* tourist trappings abound, but the springs are a true natural wonder, well worth a visit. Glass-bottom boats *(fee)* and crystalline water allow viewing of subsurface wildlife, and interpretive displays provide information about the endangered species found here, including the fountain darter (a tiny fish).

South on I-35, ❻ **New Braunfels** *(Visitors Bureau 830-625-2385 or 800-572-2626)* is another German-influenced town, established in 1845—a year earlier than Fredericksburg, which was founded by members of the same immigrants' society. Among the town's historic buildings are the **Hotel Faust** *(240 S. Seguin St. 830-625-7791)* and the **Prince Solms Inn** *(295 E. San Antonio St. 830-625-9169).* The latter is named for Prince Carl of Solms-Braunfels, the immigrants' original leader; the prince named the town for his home back in Germany.

The **Museum of Texas Handmade Furniture** *(1370 Church Hill Dr. 830-629-6504. Mem. Day–Labor Day Tues.-Sun., March–Mem. Day Wed.-Sun., Labor Day–Feb. Sat.-Sun.; adm. fee)* lives up to its name, displaying 19th-century pieces ranging from settlers' spare tables to the elegant works of serious craftspeople. New Braunfels' history is recounted at the **Sophienburg Museum and Archives** *(401 W. Coll St. 830-629-1572. Adm. fee),* located on the hill where Prince Carl intended to build a castle for his fiancée, Princess Sophie. (She never left Germany, and Carl returned to be with her.)

The first Germans to arrive here were assisted by an earlier immigrant named Ferdinand Lindheimer, who was also a pioneer in botany. (A type of prickly-pear cactus with the scientific designation *Opuntia lindheimeri* is one of many plants named for him.) The 1852 **Ferdinand Lindheimer Home** *(491 Comal St. 830-629-2943. May-Aug.Thurs.-Tues., weekends only rest of year; adm. fee)* is a fine example of a German-style Fachwerk house; many of Lindheimer's original possessions and furnishings are displayed.

Return to San Antonio on I-35.

Rafting the Guadaloupe River near New Braunfels

Gruene Acres

Now more or less a suburb of New Braunfels, the community of **Gruene** (pronounced green) was named for a German family that settled here in the 1870s. Located on the Guadalupe River, the town comprises a number of historic buildings, many of which have been restored as various tourist attractions. Most famous is the 1880s **Gruene Hall** *(1281 Gruene Rd. 830-629-5077),* a saloon and dance hall where music fans can enjoy a longneck beer and hear country acts like Delbert McClinton, Jerry Jeff Walker, and Asleep at the Wheel. Call for days and times of upcoming events, and wear your cowboy hat when you go.

45

● **360 miles** ● **3 to 5 days** ● **Year-round** ● **Texas bluebonnets, Indian paintbrush, and other wildflowers brighten roadsides in spring.** ● **Traffic can be bad on football-season Saturdays in Austin (Univ. of Texas), Waco (Baylor), and College Station (Texas A&M).**

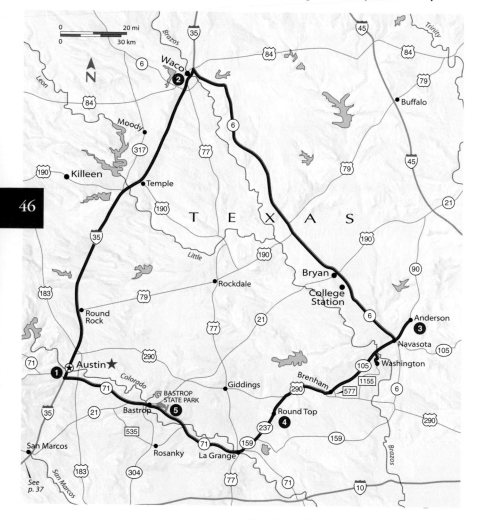

Austin, Texas' livable and human-scaled capital, is often thought of as a gateway to the famed Hill Country, which rises beyond the Balcones Escarpment to the west. This route, though, heads north and east through prairie and savanna, rolling pasture and farmland, to visit some of the state's lesser-known, but still highly rewarding, destinations. After touring the historic, cultural, and natural history sights in Austin, you'll travel to Waco, where the diverse attractions include memorials to poet Robert Browning, the Texas Rangers (the lawmen, not the baseball team), and an iconic soft drink. Then it's south to College Station, home of Texas A&M University, and Bastrop, where the "lost pines" stand as a Texas botanical oddity. Along the way you'll see not one but two presidential libraries, honoring our 36th and 41st chief executives.

❶ **Austin**★ *(Visitors Bureau, 201 E. 2nd St. 512-478-0098 or 800-926-2282)* carefully nurtures its reputation as a laid-back, good-times place, where locals spend their days in the city's pretty parks and their nights listening to country rock in the music clubs along **Sixth Street.** Don't be fooled, though: Austin knows how to take care of business, too, at an array of high-tech companies, at the huge campus of the University of Texas, and at the **Texas State Capitol** *(Congress Ave. and 11th St. 512-463-0063),* completed in 1888 with 15,000 railcar loads of Texas pink granite and limestone. The **Capitol Complex Visitors Center** *(112 E. 11th St. 512-305-8400. Tues.-Sat.),* with historical exhibits on the capitol, is housed in a castlelike building that once was the General Land Office, where short-story writer O. Henry worked in the late 1880s. Call the city Visitors Bureau for information on guided and self-guided walking tours of nearby Congress Avenue and the historic Bremond Block.

With nearly 50,000 students, the **University of Texas** *(Visitor Center, Red River St. 512-471-6498. Mon.-Fri.)* is an imposing presence in Austin. Three sites of interest on campus: The **Texas Memorial Museum** *(2400 Trinity St. 512-471-1604)* contains exhibits on geology, archaeology, and natural history, as well as the original "Goddess of Liberty" statue from the capitol dome; the **Huntington Art Gallery** in the **Ransom Center** *(21st and Guadalupe Sts. 512-471-7324)* includes a contemporary Latin American art collection.

Nightlife at Threadgill's, on Austin's Sixth Street

The most famous attraction on the UT campus is the **Lyndon Baines Johnson Library and Museum**★ *(2313 Red River St. 512-916-5136),* where visitors walk through a timeline of American history from 1908 to 1969, the years of Johnson's birth and the end of his Presidency. Born in

Texas State Capitol

the Hill Country west of Austin, Johnson led the country through the turbulent sixties; exhibits here remind visitors of civil rights protests, the Vietnam War, and LBJ's "Great Society." Among the many displays in this large museum is the Bible used on *Air Force One* to swear in Johnson as President after John F. Kennedy was shot. Gifts from foreign leaders and ordinary Americans range from carved elephant tusks to an LBJ branding iron.

Located on a hill east of the city center, the **French Legation Museum** *(802 San Marcos St. 512-472-8180. Closed Mon.; adm. fee)* centers on a house built in the 1840s by the French chargé d'affaires to the Republic of Texas. The residence, constructed in a style recalling Louisiana bayou houses, still contains furnishings of the French emissary, Alphonse Dubois de Saligny, including historic kitchen antiques. The **Elisabet Ney Museum** *(304 E. 44th St. 512-458-2255. Wed.-Sun.)* displays portrait sculptures by the fascinating and influential Ney (1833-1907), who was a successful artist in Europe before moving to the United States in the 1870s. The collection, housed in Ney's castle-like stone studio, include Texas hero Stephen F. Austin, as well such Old World figures as King Ludwig II of Bavaria. The **O. Henry Museum** *(409 E. 5th St. 512-472-1903. Wed.-Sun.)* preserves the house once occupied by William Sydney Porter, who adopted the pseudonym O. Henry and gained fame as a short-story writer after he was convicted in 1898 of embezzling from an Austin bank.

One of many fine parks in Austin, **Wild Basin Wilderness Preserve** *(805 N. Capital of Texas Hwy. 512-327-7622)* comprises 227 acres of oak-juniper woodland and grassland alongside Bee Creek; the preserve offers tours and nature programs, and more than 2 miles of trails. The **National Wildflower Research Center** ★ *(4801 La Crosse Ave. 512-292-4200. Closed Mon.; adm. fee)* was founded in 1982 by Lady Bird Johnson, LBJ's widow, and now encompasses 42 acres of Hill Country landscape. In addition to a variety of gardens, the architecturally striking center includes an exhibition gallery, an observation tower, and nature trails.

An hour north of Austin on I-35, **Temple** *(Visitors Bureau 254-298-5720)* began in 1881 as a railroad town on the Gulf, Colorado, & Santa Fe line. That heritage is the focus of the **Railroad and Pioneer Museum** *(710 Jack*

Baskin Dr. 254-298-5172. Tues.-Sat.; adm. fee), housed in a Santa Fe Railroad depot relocated from nearby Moody. A 1921 Baldwin locomotive stands outside; the depot is full of railroad artifacts, local antiques, and historical objects. Downtown, the delightful **SPJST Museum** *(520 N. Main St. 254-773-1575. Mon.-Fri.)* preserves the heritage of the influential local Czech population, whose ancestors moved to Texas in the late 19th century to escape religious and political persecution in their homeland. Housed in the basement of a Czech-founded fraternal society (its initials make up the museum's name), the collection includes traditional costumes, pioneer household items, and, of course, memorabilia of local polka bands.

➋ **Waco** *(Visitors Bureau 817-750-5810 or 800-321-9226)*, farther north on the banks of the Brazos River, can boast a widely disparate list of attractions. Consider that you can, in one afternoon, see Robert Browning's snuffbox, a fossil turtle the size of a small car, and the guns that outlaws Clyde Barrow and Bonnie Parker were carrying when they met their bloody end in 1934.

Lovers of the Old West's mystique will find plenty of boots, saddles, and guns at the **Texas Ranger Hall of Fame and Museum** *(I-35 and University Parks Dr. 254-750-8631. Adm. fee)*, honoring the lawmen who've kept order in Texas, republic and state, for more than a century and a half. The huge collection of weapons from both good guys and badmen includes Billy the Kid's Winchester 73 rifle and Bonnie and Clyde's guns. And, in case you've wondered what one looked like, the museum also exhibits a hairball from a bison. The nearby **Texas Sports**

Batty for Bats

No survey of Austin's natural scene would be complete without mentioning the famed Congress Avenue Bridge bat colony. Once a local curiosity, now a full-fledged tourist attraction, the huge congregation of Mexican free-tailed bats can number up to 1.5 million flying mammals after young are born in midsummer. The bats rest by day under the Congress Avenue Bridge over Town Lake just south of downtown, and can be seen as they leave the roost around sundown from mid-March to November. There are viewing areas on both the north and south banks of Town Lake. Call the Bat Hotline *(512-416-5700 ext. 3636)* for viewing times.

49

Four stories of presidential documents at the Lyndon Baines Johnson Library and Museum

Hall of Fame *(1108 S. University Parks Dr. 254-756-1633. Adm. fee)* will please fans with memorabilia of a long list of Texas sportsmen and women, including golfers Lee Trevino and Byron Nelson, boxer George Foreman, and all-around wonder woman Babe Didrikson Zaharias.

Housed in an impressive building on the campus of Baylor University, the **Armstrong Browning Library**★ *(Speight Ave. and 8th St. 254-710-3566. Closed Sun.)* claims the world's largest collection of materials related to English poets Robert Browning and his wife, Elizabeth Barrett Browning. In addition to books, manuscripts, artwork, and personal items, the library comprises 56 stained-glass windows illustrating the Brownings' poems, displays of Wedgwood china, and a statue of Browning's character Pippa, her countenance fully expressing her belief that "God's in His Heaven, All's right with the world." A few blocks away, Baylor's **Strecker Museum** *(817-755-1110. Closed Mon.)* includes Native American artifacts, fossils, and natural history and geological exhibits. Ask at the museum about plans to open for public visitation the site of the discovery of 24 fossil mammoths dating from 28,000 years ago; this extraordinary assemblage, of significant importance, was found within the Waco city limits. Just north of the main campus, more than 20 historic buildings have been moved to the **Gov. Bill and Vara**

Brazos River, near Waco

50

Daniel Historic Village *(1108 S. University Parks Dr. 254-710-1160. Closed Mon.; adm. fee)* to re-create a typical Texas river town of the 1890s. The village includes a cotton gin, blacksmith shop, saloon, church, and general store, all appropriately set alongside the Brazos River.

Downtown, the **Dr Pepper Museum and Free Enterprise Institute** *(300 S. 5th St. 817-757-1024. Adm. fee)* tells the story of the "King of Beverages," invented at Waco's Old Corner Drug Store in 1885. Located in a restored 1906 bottling plant, the museum recalls the early days of the soft drink industry and, for trivia fans, finally answers the burning question: Does the Dr in Dr Pepper have a period or not? (Answer: Sometimes it did, sometimes it didn't.) The 1858 **Earle-Harrison House** *(1901 N. 5th St. 254-753-2032. Adm. fee)*, a Greek Revival house built by an early Waco physician, displays antiques and period items.

From Waco, drive southeast on Tex. 6 to the twin cities of **Bryan-College Station** *(Visitor Bureau 409-260-9898 or 800-777-8292)*, home to **Texas A&M University** *(Visitor Center, Rudder Tower at Houston St. and Joe Routt Blvd. 409-845-5851)*, with nearly 50,000 students one of America's largest universities, and without a doubt possessor of the most fiercely loyal body of alumni. The **Sam Houston Sanders Corps of Cadets Center** *(Spence Park, bet. Throckmorten and Coke Sts. 409-862-2862)* on campus introduces visitors to the university's long and distinguished history. The **Forsyth Center Galleries** *(Memorial Student Center, Joe Routt Blvd. 409-845-9251)* is worth a visit for its renowned collection of art glass.

The newest attraction on the A&M campus, opened in November 1997, is the **George Bush Presidential Library and Museum ★** *(409-260-9552. Adm. fee)*, containing more than 40,000 artifacts of Bush's career not only as President but as World War II pilot, congressman, ambassador to the United Nations, director of the Central Intelligence Agency, and Vice President under Ronald Reagan. Bush's Presidency saw one of the 20th century's most momentous events in the dismantling of the Soviet empire; museum exhibits touch on that historic milestone as well as the invasion of Panama and the 1991 Persian Gulf war

Continue southeast on Tex. 6 to Tex. 90 and turn east to the small town of ❸ **Anderson,** home of **Fanthorp Inn State Historical Park** *(579 Main St. 409-873-2633. Wed.-Sun.; adm. fee)*. Built in 1834 and once a thriving stop on several stage lines, the two-story inn has been restored to its mid-19th-century appearance, with its dining table set for a meal and cards and dominoes on tables in the parlor. While you're in town you can stop to admire the remarkable 1894 **Grimes County Courthouse,** built of brick and native stone and dominating the scene from its hilltop location.

Backtrack on Tex. 90 and take Tex. 105 to Washington and **Washington-on-the-Brazos State Historical Park** *(Rte. 1155. 409-878-2214)*, where delegates met in 1836 at a tiny backwoods hamlet to declare Texas' independence from Mexico. The present park includes a reconstruction of tiny Independence Hall; the restored home of Anson Jones, last president of the Republic of Texas; and the fine **Star of the Republic Museum** *(409-878-2461)*, with exhibits on the years 1836-46, when Texas stood proudly as an independent country alongside the U.S.

Oil-drilling statue, Texas A&M University

In the pantheon of great Texas foods, Blue Bell Ice Cream ranks right at the top, alongside chili, chicken-fried steak, and barbecue. If you'd like to sample a bit of the sweet stuff and learn how it's made, stop in Brenham at **Blue Bell Creameries** *(Tex. 577, off US 290. 409-830-2197 or 800-327-8135. Mon.-Fri.; adm. fee)* for a tour. The number of visitors is limited, so call ahead. Kids will enjoy the **Monastery of St. Clare** *(9300 Tex. 105. 409-836-9652. Donation)*, a farm where nuns raise cute miniature horses that visitors can pet and photograph.

From US 290, Tex. 237 leads south to tiny ❹ **Round Top,** with its picturesque courthouse on the town square. The town's Germanic heritage is reflected in **Henkel Square** *(Main and N. Live Oak Sts. 409-249-3308. Wed.-Sun.; adm. fee)*, a collection of restored historic buildings dating from the mid-1800s, including an 1872 Lutheran church.

Go south to Tex. 71 and turn northwest to **Bastrop,** named for an immigrant politician early Texans knew as "Baron de Bastrop" of Holland—actually an imposter who had fled Europe after being accused of embezzlement. Bastrop is best known for the nearby forest known as the "lost pines," a woodland of loblollies growing 100 miles west of the Piney Woods (see Piney Woods drive, p. 62). Roads and hiking trails wind through the pines at ❺ **Bastrop State Park** *(Tex. 21 and Loop 150. 512-321-2101. Activities fees)*, which also offers golf, swimming, and camping. Car buffs should make a side trip 12 miles south on Tex. 304 to the **Central Texas Museum of Automotive History** *(Tex. 304. 512-237-2635. April-Sept. Wed.-Sun., Fri.-Sun. rest of year; adm. fee)*, displaying antique vehicles, from Edsel to Rolls-Royce.

Return to Austin via Tex. 71.

● 355 miles ● 4 to 6 days ● Year-round, though summer humidity is notoriously tropical.

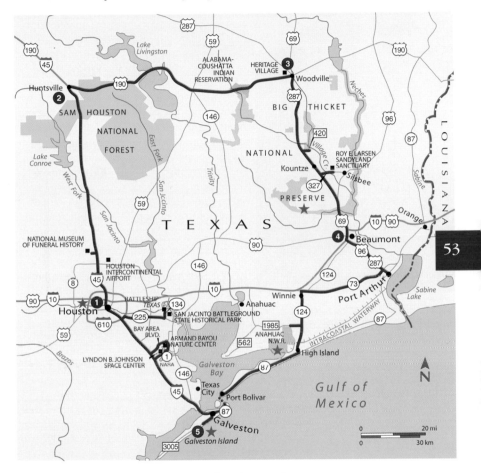

Rich, rowdy, ambitious, vain, sprawling, home of laissez-faire commerce and racetrack freeways—these are some of the stereotypes that cling to Houston, and all of them are at least partially true. But so what? Texas' biggest city (and America's fourth biggest) is large enough to contain multitudes, including a number of rich people who have done very admirable things with their money. Houston's museums include some of the country's best, and its opera company is known worldwide for excellence and innovation. Thanks to the huge National Aeronautics and Space Administration (NASA) facility here, one of the first words spoken on the moon was "Houston" (right before "the *Eagle* has landed"). Despite its headlong, oil-money-driven urge to grow, the city has maintained green spaces

54

Skyscrapers in downtown Houston

for rest and reflection. And there are probably even a few Houstonians who don't drive 90 on the freeways—though after you've been here awhile you may find this last point arguable.

There's more to this route than Houston, too. After exploring the big city a bit, the drive heads north to visit several historic sites and a Native American reservation. Then it's south to another selection of museums, and west along the Gulf Coast to the beaches and fine old houses of Galveston Island.

In a way, Texas can be said to have been born at what is now ❶ **Houston**★ *(Visitors Bureau 713-227-3100 or 800-446-8786),* since it was near here in 1836 that Sam Houston's troops defeated the far larger Mexican army of General Santa Anna and won independence from Mexico. The site of that decisive fight, the outcome of which was determined in 18 minutes, is **San Jacinto Battleground State Historical Park** *(3523 Tex. 134, N of Tex. 225, La Porte. 281-479-2431).* The 570-foot limestone **San Jacinto Monument** towers over the scene, providing a panorama of the city skyline and the busy Houston Ship Channel. At the monument's base, the **San Jacinto Museum of History** *(281-479-2421. Fees for monument elevator and audiovisual program)* presents exhibits on Texas history and an audiovisual program on the battle. Docked a short distance away, the **Battleship *Texas*** *(281-479-2431. Adm. fee)* recalls a different era of warfare. Commissioned in 1914, the restored *Texas* saw action in both World Wars, at Normandy, Iwo Jima, Okinawa, and North Africa. Visitors can roam through the crew's quarters, the bridge, and other areas.

A bronze Sam Houston sits astride a horse, pointing toward San Jacinto, in Houston's **Hermann Park** *(S. Main St. and Hermann Dr.),* a large and immensely popular downtown recreation area. Conveniently grouped within easy walking distance of this spot are some of the city's finest museums, beginning with the wonderful **Houston Museum of Natural Science**★★ *(1 Hermann Circle Dr. 713-639-4629. Adm. fee).* Just a few highlights: the six-story-high walk-through Cockrell Butterfly Center *(adm. fee)* with hundreds of brilliant species flitting through the greenery, a paleontology hall with dramatic and well-presented dinosaur displays and dioramas, Weiss Energy Hall (with an understandable emphasis on oil exploration) featuring interactive exhibits and a neon oil refinery, a renowned collection of gems and minerals, and a 63-foot Foucault pendulum that silently and impressively demonstrates that the Earth spins on its axis.

A couple of blocks away, the **Museum of Health and Medical Science** *(1515 Hermann Dr. 713-521-1515. Closed Mon.; adm. fee)* lets you look deep inside yourself in a way that has nothing to do with soul-searching. As you enter the Amazing Body Pavilion, you can walk into an open mouth or down a throat and curving esophagus into giant models of the stomach, heart, and rib cage. Inner-body explorers can then walk into a huge brain, look into an outsize eyeball, or play a video game that shows the dangers of drunk driving while participants stay safely sober.

Kids learn through playing at the **Children's Museum of Houston** *(1500 Binz St. 713-522-1138. Closed Mon.; adm. fee)*, located in a colorful building designed by Robert Venturi. They can shop for groceries (and learn which foods are healthy) in a child-size store, create their own art masterpieces, discover how telephones work, see what makes a house energy-efficient, stand inside a soap bubble, and lots of other "messy fun stuff."

It's just a short walk to the **Museum of Fine Arts, Houston**★ *(1001 Bissonnet St. 713-639-7300. Closed Mon.; adm. fee)*, where paintings by Seurat, Renoir, Cassatt, Monet, Cézanne, Gauguin, and van Gogh, sculptures by Rodin, Matisse, and Giacometti, and fabulous exhibits of African and Indonesian gold highlight an extensive collection. Also in this classy neighborhood: the **Contemporary Arts Museum** *(5216 Montrose Blvd. 713-284-8250. Closed Mon.)*, a noncollecting museum that hosts changing

Orange Show

Ranking at the top of the list of Houston's quirkiest and most engaging attractions, the **Orange Show** *(2401 Munger St. 713-926-6368. Mid-March–Mem. Day and Labor Day–mid-Dec. weekends, Mem. Day–Labor Day Wed. and Fri.-Sun.; adm. fee)* is like a crazy, colorful maze of exuberantly decorated...stuff. Put together from tile, awnings, wheels, umbrellas, flags, and sundry other attention-getting bric-a-brac, the folk-art masterpiece is the result of 25 years of labor by an eccentric Houstonian whose goal was to "encourage people to eat oranges, drink oranges, and be highly amused." On the last point, he definitely succeeded. Go and see for yourself.

55

Halftime at Houston's Astrodome

exhibitions of contemporary art, and **Holocaust Museum Houston** *(5401 Caroline St. 713-942-8000)*, which in a strikingly designed building presents exhibits on that tragic episode of history, as well as a video with local Holocaust survivors recounting their experiences.

The **Menil Collection**★ *(1515 Sul Ross St. 713-525-9400. Wed.-Sun.)* is another of the city's major arts attractions, displaying the extensive collection of a wealthy local couple who concentrated on four main areas: antiquities; Byzantine and medieval art; tribal art of Africa, Oceania, and the Pacific Northwest; and 20th-century art. The museum has the world's largest collection of art by Max Ernst and René Magritte, and also includes Picasso, Rothko, Calder, and Klee. (The Menil building, designed by Renzo Piano, architect of the Centre Pompidou in Paris, is a superb environment in which to see art.) Just across the street is the Menil's **Cy Twombly Gallery** *(1501 Branard St. Wed.-Sun.)*, and down the street stands **Rothko Chapel**★ *(1409 Sul Ross St.)*, in which 14 large-scale paintings by Mark Rothko—dark, subdued, even somber—combine with natural lighting and the octagonal interior to create an aura of peace and contemplation.

Saturn V rocket at Lyndon B. Johnson Space Center

Farther west, **Bayou Bend Collection and Gardens**★ *(1 Westcott St. 713-639-7750. Closed Mon.; separate fees for house and gardens)* centers on the mansion of a woman with the marvelous name of Ima Hogg, the daughter of a Texas governor, who spent many of her 93 years of life collecting American art, antiques, furniture, and decorative objects. Works by Duncan Phyfe, Charles Willson Peale, and Paul Revere adorn the 28 rooms of Bayou Bend; outside, 14 acres comprise 8 gardens in differing styles.

The closest most people will ever come to outer space will probably be about 20 miles southeast of downtown Houston, at **Space Center Houston**★★ *(1601 NASA Rd. 1. 281-244-2100 or 800-972-0369. Adm. fee)*, the Visitor Center for NASA's **Lyndon B. Johnson Space Center.** Here visitors can listen to live communications between Mission

Control and the space shuttle (if there's one currently in orbit), tour a model of the shuttle and pretend to land one, see historic spacecraft such as the Apollo 17 command module, and get close-up looks at space suits and moon rocks. A special area lets kids experience the moon's low gravity and play astronaut in a variety of interactive exhibits. A tram tour travels through Johnson Space Center, with displays of rockets and actual astronaut-training areas.

After seeing all this high-tech gadgetry, people who'd like to get back in touch with Mother Earth can make the short drive to **Armand Bayou Nature Center** *(8500 Bay Area Blvd. 281-474-2551. Wed.-Sun.; adm. fee)*, where trails wind around and through prairie, wetland, and woods, and exhibits explain the ecology of the Texas coast. And for those willing to try something a bit unconventional, the **National Museum of Funeral History** *(415 Barren Springs Dr. 281-876-3063. Adm. fee)*, north of the city near Houston Intercontinental Airport, provides an intriguing look at the history of last rites, including a Funerals of the Famous exhibit. The most entertaining part is a collection of funeral vehicles, from horse-drawn hearses to elaborate motorized conveyances.

South of Huntsville along I-45, a 67-foot statue of Sam Houston lets travelers know they're near the homestead of this hero of Texas independence: the general who defeated Santa Anna in 1836; president of the Republic of Texas; U.S. senator; and state governor, who finally fell from power for refusing to support the Confederacy when Texas seceded from the Union. In ❷ **Huntsville,** on the campus of Sam Houston State University, the **Sam Houston Memorial Museum** *(1836 Sam Houston Ave. 409-294-1832. Closed Mon.)* encompasses a number of Houston-related attractions, all of them on the site of what was once his farm. Houston built his dogtrot-style Woodland Home in 1848 and lived in it for ten years; nearby stands a one-room cabin that was his law office. The 1850s Steamboat House, where Houston died in 1863, has been moved here from a nearby location. Many Houston artifacts are displayed in the adjacent Exhibit Hall, including the copper plate used to print his calling cards (which read simply, "Sam Houston, Texas"), and personal items of defeated Mexican General Santa Anna. (The ignominy of defeat: Your chamberpot is put on public display for posterity.)

Follow US 190 eastward to the **Alabama-Coushatta Indian Reservation** *(409-563-4391 or 800-444-3507. June-Aug. daily, March-May and Sept.-Nov. Fri.-Sun., closed Dec.-Feb.; adm. fee)*, established in 1854 with the help of Sam Houston, who wanted to reward the two tribes for their

For the Birds

High Island *(Bolivar Peninsula Chamber of Commerce 409-684-5940 or 800-FUN-SUN-3)* is a name that rings in a birdwatcher's ear the way Lincoln Center does for music lovers, or Pebble Beach for golfers. The trees in this tiny coastal town east of Galveston—the only significant woodland for miles around—act as an irresistible attractant for small birds crossing the Gulf of Mexico northward during spring migration. When bad weather creates a "fallout" of birds along the coast, High Island's woods can be an outdoor aviary of warblers, vireos, thrushes, tanagers, orioles, and other species. Late April is the peak time, when the town is crowded with binocular-toting birders hoping for a glimpse of a Cape May warbler or a veery.

neutrality in the war with Mexico. Tribal members lead tours through natural woodland, perform traditional dances, and demonstrate crafts at the **Living Indian Village.** A short distance farther east, ❸ **Heritage Village** *(US 190. 409-283-2272. Adm. fee)* is a collection of old-time buildings, some original and others reconstructed, that re-create a 19th-century small town. Antique furnishings, tools, and commercial items fill structures including a blacksmith shop, post office, and saloon.

Take US 69/287 south into the heart of the Big Thicket, a region of pines, savanna, and swampy woods that once covered more than three million acres of East Texas. Today, **Big Thicket National Preserve★** *(Visitor Information Station 409-246-2337)* protects around 86,000 acres in several scattered tracts, comprising one of Texas' most ecologically significant and diverse natural areas. The preserve offers many miles of hiking trails, but for a quick introduction, stop by the Visitor Information Station on Rte. 420 north of Kountze and walk the 1.7-mile **Kirby Nature Trail.** In a short time here visitors can experience varied habitats and lush plant life, from bald cypress and swamp cyrilla in the floodplain to beech and southern magnolia on the higher slopes. A bit farther south, the Nature Conservancy manages the **Roy E. Larsen Sandyland Sanctuary** *(Tex. 327, W of Silsbee. 409-385-4135),* a micro-cosm of the Big Thicket, where trails wind alongside pretty Village Creek.

At ❹ **Beaumont,** the **Tourist Information Center** *(Off I-10 at Martin Luther King St. exit. 409-833-4622)* also serves as a mini-museum of local heroine Babe Didrikson Zaharias, with trophies, golf clubs, tennis rackets, and other memo-rabilia from the almost literally incredi-ble career of the greatest woman athlete of all time. This is also the best place to pick up information on things to see and do in the region known as the Golden Triangle, formed by Beaumont, Port Arthur, and Orange, where the Sabine River meets the Gulf of Mexico.

It was black gold that thoroughly transformed the area beginning on Jan-uary 10, 1901, when the biggest oil field ever found spewed crude all around a low hill called Spindletop, just south of Beaumont. The city's population went

Swamp at Big Thicket National Preserve

from 10,000 to 50,000 in less than two years; great fortunes were made, and companies such as Texaco, Gulf, and Mobil were born in the rush to drill. **Spindletop/ Gladys City Boomtown Museum** *(US 69 and University Dr. 409-835-0823. Closed Mon.; adm. fee)* is a re-creation of one of the towns that sprang up near Spindletop. Buildings, clustered around a tall derrick, contain original equipment from the boom days. For more on the oil business, visit the **Texas Energy Museum**★ *(600 Main St. 409-833-5100. Closed Mon.; adm. fee)*, which begins at the very beginning (the origin of the universe) to tell the story of petroleum, how it originated, how it's found, and how it's used. The

Texas Energy Museum, Beaumont

language is sometimes a little technical, but the exhibits— from giant models of hydrocarbon molecules to talking robotic figures—are lively and entertaining.

Beaumont's McFaddin family was already rich when the Spindletop gusher came in, and their part-ownership of land in the well area made them even richer. See the kind of lifestyle their money got them at the **McFaddin-Ward House**★ *(1906 Calder Ave. 409-832-2134 Closed Mon.; adm. fee)*; the home was built in 1906 in the beaux arts-colonial style, an ornate concoction of columns, railings, spindles, and dormers. Furnishings and personal items in the grand interior include fine woodwork, chandeliers, glassware, and Oriental rugs. After seeing the main house, tour the 1907 carriage house, with its gymnasium, stable, and displays on the lives of servants of the era.

Only in the context of **Port Arthur** would the names of singer Janis Joplin, artist Robert Rauschenberg, and football coach Jimmy Johnson be used in the same sentence. The disparate trio grew up in the area, and their stories are part of the **Museum of the Gulf Coast** *(701 4th St. 409-982-7000. Adm. fee)*, which reflects its comprehensive title with a collection ranging from Native American artifacts to decorative glassware to a room honoring sports heroes. In the music room there's a reproduction of Joplin's hippie-psychedelic Porsche and a high school yearbook showing that she was a member of the Slide Rule Club. But she wasn't the only musician from these parts: The museum also includes displays on Tex Ritter, the Big Bopper, Johnny and Edgar Winter, Clarence "Gatemouth" Brown, and many others.

Take Tex. 73 west toward Winnie, then Tex. 124 south toward the Gulf. Nature lovers will want to make the side

Strand National Historic Landmark District, Galveston Island

trip west on Rte. 1985 to **Anahuac National Wildlife Refuge**★ *(409-267-3337)*, 33,000 acres of marsh and ponds where alligators, wading birds, and waterfowl abound. It can be hot, humid, and buggy in summer, but it's a birdwatcher's paradise anytime.

At High Island (see sidebar p. 57), take Tex. 87 to Port Bolivar and ride the free ferry *(409-763-2386)* across to ❺ **Galveston Island**★ *(Convention & Visitors Bureau, 2102 Seawall Blvd. 409-763-4311 or 800-GAL-ISLE)*. With hundreds of notable buildings, it's one of Texas' most historic places, and with 32 miles of beaches it's certainly one of the state's most popular playgrounds. Trade at Galveston's port created great wealth in the 19th century, but a hurricane in 1900 pushed the Gulf waters completely across the low island, killing 6,000 people and ending the city's economic glory days. A legacy of that tragedy is a 10-mile-long **seawall** begun in 1904, today a great place to ride a bike, jog, or just stroll along watching the surf roll in.

Exhibits at the **Galveston County Historical Museum** *(2219 Market St. 409-766-2340)* recount the island's past from the days of the Karankawa and Atakapa Indians through the years when the business district was known as the Wall Street of the Southwest and into the 20th century. The museum is located on the edge of the "Wall Street" area, now called the **Strand National Historic Landmark District** *(Visitor Center, 2016 Strand. 409-765-7834)*, a tourist area full of restored 19th-century buildings. Nearby, the **Railroad Museum**★ *(123 25th St. 409-765-5700. Adm. fee)*, at the city's 1932 Santa Fe depot, displays more than 40 restored railcars, watched over by actual-size sculptures depicting old-time travelers. At Pier 21, the **Texas Seaport Museum** *(409-763-1877. Adm. fee)* focuses on Galveston's legacy as one of the nation's most important ports, but its best attraction floats outside: The tall ship ***Elissa***, a square-rigged sailing craft built in Scotland in 1877, has been restored to its original appearance; visitors can explore its shipshape exterior and cabins. The beautifully restored **Grand 1894 Opera House** *(2020 Postoffice St. 409-765-1894 or 800-821-1894),* located just outside the landmark district, has hosted Sarah Bernhardt and Lillian Russell and continues to offer live performances today.

The island's 19th-century affluence built a great many fine houses, some of which are open for tours. The 1886 **Bishop's Palace**★ *(1402 Broadway. 409-762-2475. Adm. fee)* is noted for its splendid fireplaces around which the first owner, Col. Walter Gresham, designed the rooms. In 1923 the palace became the residence of the local Catholic bishop. The elegant woodwork, including rosewood, satinwood, and white mahogany, graces an interior of nearly staggering sumptuousness. The 1859 Italianate **Ashton Villa** *(2328 Broadway. 409-762-3933. Adm. fee)* features intricate ironwork, fine antiques, and memorabilia of its first owner, James Moreau Brown, one of Texas' wealthiest businessmen. **Moody Mansion**★ *(2618 Broadway. 409-762-7668. Closed Mon. Jan.-March; adm. fee)* was built about 1895 and bought after the 1900 hurricane by William L. Moody, Jr., a member of one of Texas' most prominent and successful families. The limestone and redbrick house contains handsome hand-carved woodwork and plaster decorative details, as well as appropriately luxurious furnishings.

The **David Taylor Classic Car Museum** *(1918 Mechanic St. 409-765-6590. Adm. fee)* concentrates on American classics, from horseless carriages to big-engine "muscle cars" of the sixties, while the **Lone Star Flight Museum** *(2002 Terminal Dr. at Scholes Field, Galveston Municipal Airport. 409-740-7722. Adm. fee)* displays more than 40 restored airplanes. **Moody Gardens' Rainforest Pyra-**

At Moody Gardens' Rainforest Pyramid

mid *(409-744-4673 or 800-582-4673. 1 Hope Blvd. Adm. fee)* has over 2,000 species of plants, animals, and tropical fish.

Return to Houston via I-45.

● **260 miles** ● **3 to 4 days** ● **Year-round**

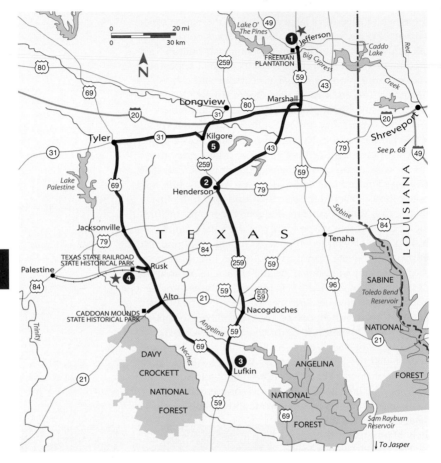

Timber, cotton, steamboats, railroads, and oil all contributed to the development of northeastern Texas, a region that saw its first European settlements along El Camino Real, the "royal road" that ran from San Antonio to Louisiana in the late 17th- and 18th-century days of Spanish colonization. Much of the area is covered by pines, the western extension of the great conifer forest that stretches from the Atlantic to East Texas—and that still provides the raw material for sawmills and paper plants in the land Texans call the Piney Woods. No metropolis dominates this part of the state, but several small cities offer fine museums and historic sites; state parks include Native American ceremonial mounds and an old-time railroad line.

The route begins in history-rich Jefferson, then heads south to Nacogdoches, where in 1716 a Spanish mission was established at the site of a Nacogdoche Indian village. After continuing southward to Lufkin, home of a museum honoring the local timber industry, the drive loops back north to Tyler, with a fine zoo and rose garden, and Kilgore, where a fascinating museum tells the story of the East Texas oil field and the boom it ignited in the 1930s.

Steamboat traffic made ❶ **Jefferson** ★ *(Chamber of Commerce 903-665-2672)* Texas' largest inland port in the mid-19th century; boats took away cotton and timber and brought in supplies for a thriving commercial city. Improvements to navigation on the Red River in 1873 lowered the water level of Big Cypress Bayou, and the town, too, began a slow decline. Today, Jefferson attracts visitors eager to see buildings from the glory days or stay in a historic B&B.

The **Jefferson Historical Society Museum** *(223 W. Austin St. 903-665-2775. Adm. fee)* houses a vast miscellany in a massive brick structure begun in 1888 as the post office and federal courthouse. Spread over five levels, the collection is full of minor treasures, from old medical devices to Confederate money. Just down the street, the **Excelsior House** *(211 W. Austin St. 903-665-2513. Fee for tours)* has been in continuous operation as a hotel since the 1850s and offers afternoon tours of the public areas and antique-filled rooms. Past guests have included Ulysses S. Grant, Oscar Wilde, and railroad tycoon Jay Gould, who (the story goes) wrote "End of Jefferson Texas" in the register

63

Harrison County Historical Museum, Marshall

after the town turned down his offer to bring in a rail line. Gould's private railcar, the ***Atalanta*** *(Fee for tour; tickets at Excelsior House)*, sits just across the street. Mahogany and maple woodwork embellishes two observation rooms, four staterooms, and a bath—part of the perks of being a 19th-century "robber baron."

The **House of the Seasons** ★ *(409 S. Alley St. 903-665-1218. Call for tour times; fee for tours)* was built in 1872 in a combination of Greek Revival, Victorian, and Italianate styles. Panels of stained glass at the top of a central rotunda symbolize the seasons of the year; furnishings include ornate chandeliers and an 1876 Knabe piano. The 1860 **Beard House** *(212 Vale St. 903-665-2606. Closed Wed. and Sun.; fee for tours)*, built of bald cypress and pine, has 14-foot ceilings and the original detached kitchen still standing. Just west of town, the 1850 **Freeman Plantation** *(Tex. 49. 903-665-2320. Closed Wed.; fee for tours)* was constructed of handmade bricks and bald cypress, with four large columns supporting the front gallery.

Head south on US 59 to **Marshall** *(Chamber of Commerce 903-935-7868).* Here, the **Harrison County Historical Museum** *(Washington and Houston Sts. 903-938-2680. Tues.-Sat.; adm. fee)* is located in the fancifully decorated old county courthouse, built in 1901. Inside are exhibits on famous natives (e.g. boxer George Foreman and broadcaster Bill Moyers), Caddo Indians, the Civil War, and other historical nuggets. A few blocks to the southwest, **Starr Family State Historical Park** *(407 W. Travis St. 903-935-3044. Sat.-Sun.; fee for tours)* comprises several historic structures, some of which were occupied by Starr family members from 1870 until 1985. Maplecroft, the large home at the center of the park, was built in the Italianate style in 1870 and remodeled as a Greek Revival house in the 1920s; all furnishings are original. Marshall is also known for pottery; the largest local factory, **Marshall Pottery** *(4901 Elysian Fields Rd. 903-938-9201),* puts out ten million red-clay pots a year and offers demonstrations in its large retail outlet.

Take Tex. 43 southwest to ❷ **Henderson** *(Chamber of Commerce 903-657-5528),* home of the **Depot Museum Complex** *(514 N. High St. 903-657-4303. Closed Sun.; adm. fee),* a noteworthy grouping of historic buildings centered on a 1901 Missouri Pacific depot. Other structures include a board-and-batten dogtrot, an 1841 log cabin with authentic period furnishings, and a barn full of old farm tools. The museum also claims the only outhouse with an official Texas historical marker, a fancy 1908 three-holer.

Faced with the threat of French expansion into its territory, Spain built a line of presidios and missions in East Texas around the turn of the 18th century; after decades of sometimes tenuous existence, these missions were given orders to be abandoned in 1773. A group of

Depot Museum Complex in Henderson

64

homesick settlers led by Don Antonio Gil Y'Barbo eventually returned to the region, founding what was to become the city of **Nacogdoches** *(Visitors Bureau 409-564-7351)* in 1779. Here Y'Barbo built a stone house; though it was torn down in 1902, the original stones were used to rebuild the house in 1936 on the campus of Stephen F. Austin State University. Today it stands as the **Stone Fort Museum** *(Alumni Dr. and Griffith Blvd. 409-468-2408. Closed Mon.)*, with exhibits on regional history, especially the period from the first Spanish mission of 1690 to Texas independence in 1836.

Period room at Millard's Crossing Historic Village, Nacogdoches

North of the city, a fine collection of venerable structures from around Nacogdoches County has been gathered at **Millard's Crossing Historic Village** *(6020 North St. 409-564-6631. Fee for tours)*, where tours visit an 1837 boardinghouse, a 1905 chapel, and five other historic buildings; furnishings and artifacts range from elegant antiques to a shed full of great old gadgets. The **Sterne-Hoya House** *(211 S. Lanana St. 409-560-5426. Closed Sun.)* was built about 1830 by Adolphus Sterne, a German immigrant who took an active part in the Texas Revolution; it was later sold to Joseph von der Hoya, a Prussian settler. One parlor has been restored and furnished to reflect Sterne's milieu, while another depicts von der Hoya's Victorian era.

When the first Europeans arrived in East Texas, they found up to 18 million acres of virgin pinewoods.

❸ **Lufkin,** south on US 59, has long been a center for the timber industry that grew up to exploit that resource, a heritage preserved in the city's **Texas Forestry Museum** *(1905 Atkinson Dr. 409-632-9535)*. Outside stand a 100-foot fire tower, a 1908 steam locomotive, and other pieces of mechanized logging equipment. Inside are memorabilia from mill towns, exhibits on products made from wood, more old vehicles, and evocative photos from the pioneer days of forestry.

Turn north now on US 69 to Alto, then take Tex. 21 (which generally follows the route of El Camino Real) 6 miles southwest to **Caddoan Mounds State Historical Park** *(409-858-3218. Fri.-Mon.; adm. fee)*. A small museum displays tools, pots, and other artifacts of the Caddo Indians, who occupied this site from about A.D. 800 to 1300. A diorama of village life and a video presentation help visitors appreciate the highly developed civilization of the Caddo, which once dominated this region of North America. Take a short walking trail outside, through the old village area (of which little trace remains) past burial and temple mounds; excavations have provided important clues about what is now known to have been one of the

Pine forest north of Jasper

most sophisticated early Native American cultures in Texas.

Back on US 69, continue northward to Rusk and go west on US 84 a short distance to ❹ **Texas State Railroad State Historical Park**★ *(903-683-2561. June-July Thurs.-Sun., March-May and Aug.-Oct. weekends; fare for train)*. This unique state park operates steam-locomotive-drawn trains along a 25-mile route between Rusk and Palestine, passing through pinewoods and bottomland hardwoods along the way. Begun as a prison project in 1896, the line underwent several transformations before its dedication as a historical attraction in 1976; today, trains leave Rusk and Palestine simultaneously for a four-hour round-trip excursion. The steam locomotives date from 1901 to 1917, while many of the passenger cars were built in the 1920s.

A blight that destroyed Smith County's peaches early in the 1900s caused local farmers to switch to roses; the flower is now so widely cultivated and packaged that **Tyler** *(Visitors Bureau 903-592-1661 or 800-235-5712)* calls itself America's "Rose Capital." A significant number of the country's commercial rose bushes once originated in the county, and Tyler's veneration of the plant is still so great that its annual October Rose Festival has grown into a Mardi Gras-like gala. Several hundred varieties of rose are grown at the **Tyler Rose Garden** *(420 Rose Park Dr. 903-531-1213)*, with a Heritage Garden area comprising types dating back to the mid-19th century. The garden's **Tyler Rose Museum** *(903-597-3130. Closed Mon.; adm. fee)* covers all aspects of roses, with videos on the history of its cultivation and computer displays of rose varieties.

The **Caldwell Zoo** *(2203 Martin Luther King Blvd. 903-593-0121)* is superb for a city Tyler's size, well worth a look for its nicely designed exhibits. The East African section houses elephants, zebras, and rare black rhinos; the Texas area is home to bison, pronghorn, sandhill cranes, and other regional species. The zoo doesn't try to do too much for the space it has, and it's a pleasure to visit. A wide range of animals (of the deceased variety) is the main attraction at **Brookshire's World of Wildlife Museum and Country Store** *(Rte. 323 and Old Jacksonville Hwy. 903-534 2169. Tues.-Sat.)*, developed by the founder of a chain of grocery stores and his wife, both avid hunters. Mounted animals from polar bears to cottontails are shown in well-presented displays, along with extensive collections of game fish and waterfowl. In the same building is a delightful reproduction of a 1920s grocery store.

The **Goodman Museum** *(624 N. Broadway. 903-531-1286. Wed.-Sun.)* has as its centerpiece an imposing house originally built in 1859, though its present Greek Revival appearance dates from remodeling in the 1920s. Occupied for many years by a Tyler physician and his family, the home was a social center for the city and still contains original furnishings; from ornate bedrooms suites to hand-painted china, these bits of local history give the place an intimate, personal feeling.

On October 3, 1930, a wild gusher blew in at the Daisy Bradford No. 3 well in Rusk County, setting off a drilling boom at what was proclaimed the "greatest oil field in the world." In ❺ **Kilgore,** the excellent **East Texas Oil Museum**★ *(US 259 at Ross St., Kilgore College. 903-983-8295. Closed Mon.; adm. fee)* tells the story of those frenzied days, when speculators and roughnecks flooded the region, and the Texas Rangers had to be called in to keep the peace. A realistic, life-size boomtown street is populated with talking figures who relate the news of the day, and an elevator ride descends (or seems to) 3,800 feet into the earth to the Woodbine Sandstone formation, where all that black gold lies. Be sure to catch the historical movie showing at the theater.

Downtown, at the **World's Richest Acre** *(Commerce and Main Sts.)*, a mini-forest of 12 restored derricks provides a sample of the scene in the 1940s, when Kilgore had about 1,100 wells pumping oil—a time when the entire national petroleum requirement could have been met simply by the city's wells.

Return to Jefferson via I-20 and US 59.

The One and Only

Of Texas' 254 counties, one is named for a woman—or rather, named for a river that was named for a woman. Though many legends have become entwined with her tale, the central story begins in the late 17th century, when Spain was establishing its first missions in East Texas. Franciscan priests at one settlement took in a Hasinai Indian girl whom they called Angelina, "little angel." Adopted and educated by the missionaries, she learned Spanish, studied the Bible, and helped them spread their religion among local Native American tribes. The priests called her settlement "Angelina's village," a name later given to a nearby river, and, eventually, to Angelina County.

Tyler Rose Garden

Red River Ramble

● **390 miles** ● **3 to 4 days** ● **Year-round**

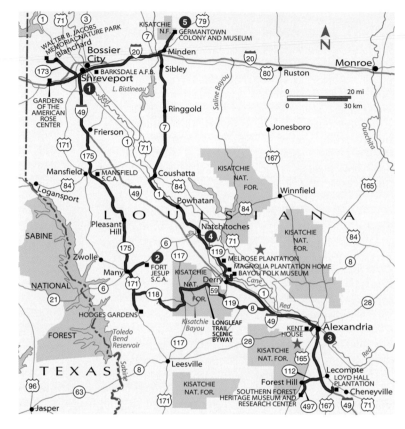

Claimed by France and Spain, fought over by Union and Confederate Armies, part Old South plantation and part urban bustle, northern Louisiana has long been a meeting ground of disparate cultures. Reminders of the past are everywhere on this drive as it loops through rolling pinewoods and flat Red River bottomlands. Just to read the names of places along the way—Caddo Parish, Fort St. Jean Baptiste, Magnolia Plantation, Germantown Colony—is to get a sense of the region's varied heritage.

The route begins with Shreveport and its cross-river neighbor, Bossier City; historic sites and an excellent botanic garden come next, before a visit to Louisiana's only national forest. After stops in and near Alexandria, including several fine old plantation houses, the drive heads back north to Natchitoches, a town with the singular distinction of being the oldest permanent European settlement in the Louisiana Purchase.

With an economy based in part on oil, gas, and

timber, **❶ Shreveport** *(Tourist Bureau 318-222-9391 or 800-551-8682)* is today the major city in the three-state area called the Ark-La-Tex; its downtown, on the bank of the Red River, has been the focus of a recent revitalization effort that encompasses museums, restaurants, and businesses. Regional history and the local environment are among the subjects covered by the **Sci-Port Discovery Center** *(Commerce and Milam Sts. 318-424-3466. Adm. fee. Moving to Clyde Fant Pkwy. and Lake St. in summer 1998)*, featuring interactive exhibits on science, health, and technology, with special areas for kids. Nearby, the **Ark-La-Tex Antique and Classic Vehicle Museum and Shreveport Firefighter's Museum** *(601 Spring St. 318-222-0227. Adm. fee)* displays fire engines, old motor scooters, early automobiles, and 1960s "muscle cars" in an oft-restored building that once housed an auto assembly area and showroom. The **Spring Street Historical Museum** *(525 Spring St. 318-424-0964. Fri.-Sun. and Tues.; adm. fee),* located in a former bank building dating from 1865, contains a collection of Civil War artifacts and furniture, clothing, and household items reflecting the lifestyle of the early settlers of northwest Louisiana.

Certainly ranking near the top of Shreveport's attractions, the **R. W. Norton Art Gallery**★ *(4747 Creswell Ave. 318-865-4201. Closed Mon.)* was founded by the son and widow of one of the discoverers of northern Louisiana's Rodessa oil field. The eclectic collection includes (to touch on just a few highlights) paintings and sculptures by Western artists Frederic Remington and Charles M.

69

Downtown Shreveport

Gardens of the American Rose Center, near Shreveport

Russell, Paul Revere silver, Rodin bronzes, a large array of Wedgwood china, an original double-elephant folio of John James Audubon's *Birds of America,* 16th-century Flemish tapestries, and paintings by American landscape artists Thomas Moran, Thomas Cole, and Albert Bierstadt. Outside, a grand azalea garden brightens the museum's 40-acre grounds in early spring. **Meadows Museum of Art at Centenary College** *(2911 Centenary Blvd. 318-869-5169. Closed Mon.)* is known for a collection of paintings and drawings of Indochina done in the 1930s by the French artist Jean Despujols. The beautifully detailed works document daily life in what was then a very remote and seldom-seen part of the world; they're well worth an afternoon's visit.

Ten miles west of Shreveport off I-20, the **Gardens of the American Rose Center** *(8877 Jefferson-Paige Rd. 318-938-5402. April-Oct. daily, late Nov.-Dec. evenings; adm. fee)* comprise 60 individual gardens within a 118-acre site operated by the American Rose Society. Spring and fall are the peak blooming times for the gardens, which show off more than 400 kinds of roses, from miniatures to antique varieties to new hybrids. For a closer look at northwestern Louisiana's outdoors, take the short drive north on La. 173 to **Walter B. Jacobs Memorial Nature Park** *(8012 Blanchard-Furrh Rd., 3 miles W of Blanchard. 318-929-2806. Wed.-Sun.),* one of the state's best nature centers. Five miles of trails wind through 160 acres of bottomland-hardwood forest, upland pines, and rolling meadows; an interpretive center helps you identify some of the plants you'll see on your explorations.

Across the river in Bossier City, the **Eighth Air Force Museum** *(Off North Gate Rd. at Barksdale Air Force Base. 318-456-3067)* looks at the role of the Eighth Air Force in and out of war, with exhibits covering combat missions as well as peacetime training; films are shown in a copy of a World War II briefing room. Outside the museum is a 9-acre display area with 17 historic planes, including a legendary P-51 Mustang and a Russian MiG-21 of the Vietnam era.

Leaving the Shreveport-Bossier City area now, drive south on I-49 to La. 175 and follow it to **Mansfield State Commemorative Area** *(15149 La. 175. 318-872-1474 or 888-677-6267. Adm. fee),* the site of the climactic battle of

What's In A Name?

You hear the term Creole everywhere in Louisiana but what, exactly, does it mean? Originally, Creole referred to those born in the colonies to European parents. More specifically, within Louisiana, Creoles are those descended from or culturally related to the children born to European parents in the Louisiana Territory after 1803. The term also refers to the descendants of blacks born in the Western Hemisphere, as opposed to those brought here from Africa. In addition, Creoles are anyone of mixed European and African ancestry. A definition popular among Cane River Creoles at least has the advantage of brevity: "We speak French, eat Spanish, and everybody's Catholic."

the Union Army's Red River Campaign in the latter stages of the Civil War. Federal troops were attempting to reach Texas by way of Shreveport and the Red River, but on April 8, 1864, Confederate forces won a decisive victory, forcing the invaders to turn back toward New Orleans. A quarter-mile walking trail crosses the main battleground; the museum has a fine collection of artifacts, including a rare Confederate 6-pounder cannon. Continue south on La. 175 and at Many, take La. 6 east to ❷ **Fort Jesup State Commemorative Area** *(32 Geoghagan Rd. 318-256-4117 or 888-677-5378. Adm. fee).* Here, Zachary Taylor commanded (in two different decades) a post built in 1822 and charged with keeping the peace in what was then an untamed and often violent land in dispute between the U.S., Spain, and Mexico. One kitchen, built of squared timbers, and stone pillars are all that remain of the original complex of 82 buildings; a museum housed in the reconstructed officers' quarters recounts the fort's history.

Return to Many and drive 16 miles south on US 171 to **Hodges Gardens** *(318-586-3523 or 800-354-3523. Adm. fee),* which in its 4,700 acres combines formal gardens, natural areas, greenhouses, and 10 miles of scenic drives. Tulips, camellias, azaleas, dogwoods, and dozens of other types of flowers bloom nearly throughout the year; the gardens also offer a fishing lake, hiking trails, and picnic areas.

The route now backtracks a few miles and follows La. 118 and La. 117 to the **Longleaf Trail Scenic Byway** (Forest Service Rd. 59), a 17-mile drive through a rugged

Towering trees at the Mansfield State Commemorative Area

section of **Kisatchie National Forest** *(318-352-2568)*. The varied topography here was produced in part by the erosive action of streams on the sedimentary rock underlying the Kisatchie Hills. The byway crosses pretty little Kisatchie Bayou, winds through forests of impressive longleaf pine, and pauses at Longleaf Vista, where the view takes in a pine-covered landscape interspersed with rock outcrops.

At La. 119, turn south and take La. 8 and I-49 to ❸ **Alexandria** *(Visitors Bureau 318-443-7049 or 800-742-7049)*, where your first stop should be the **Kent House** ★ *(3601 Bayou Rapides Rd. 318-487-5998. Adm. fee)*, the oldest extant structure in central Louisiana and an excellent recreation of antebellum plantation life. Begun in 1794 and completed in 1796, the original house was built on piers of brick made from local red clay (the handprint of a slave can still be seen in one brick); the framework is hand-hewn bald cypress with walls of *bousillage,* a mixture of mud, animal hair, and Spanish moss. In the 1840s a later owner made Greek Revival-style additions. All furnishings in Kent House date from before 1855, and its outbuildings include a detached kitchen, barn, blacksmith shop, and a sugarhouse, where the process of making sugar from cane is demonstrated each fall.

Downtown, the **Hotel Bentley** *(200 DeSoto St. 318-448-9600 or 800-356-6835)*, built in 1908 by a wealthy local lumberman and once called the "Waldorf of the Red River," has been beautifully restored after once closing (like so many of America's historic hotels) in the wake of the inner city's decline and the rise of suburban motels; stop in to see the glittering lobby with its gray marble columns, tile floor, crystal chandeliers, and marble fish pool. Like the Bentley, **Loyd Hall Plantation** *(292 Loyd Bridge Rd., off US 167. 318-776-5641 or 800-240-8135. Fee for tours)*, located just north of Cheneyville, went through a period of neglect—a much longer one, during which the house served as a glorified storehouse and barn. Today the early 19th-century home, which combines federal and Georgian styles, features original woodwork and ornate plaster moldings, as well as a collection of fine antiques. It's the center of a working farm, and guests can stay in original outbuildings.

Backtrack to La. 112 at Lecompte, and go west to Forest Hill; then drive south on La. 497 to the **Southern Forest Heritage Museum and Research Center** *(318-748-8404. Adm. fee)*, a site dedicated to the forest products industry of the great southern pinewoods. Here a complete sawmill complex, founded before the turn of the century and once employing more than 500 workers, has been preserved nearly as it was when it shut down in

1969: Tools lie on tables, lumber awaits delivery, and huge old locomotives loom impressive even in their rusty dotage. The museum is young, but has enormous potential.

Return to I-49, drive north past Alexandria to the Derry

Melrose Plantation

exit, and follow signs to the **Bayou Folk Museum** *(La. 1, Cloutierville. 318-379-2233. Adm. fee),* also known as the **Kate Chopin Home.** The two-story building, completed around 1809, contains memorabilia of the Creole culture that developed in the 19th century along the Cane River south of Natchitoches. For a few years beginning in 1879, the house was also the home of writer Kate Chopin, whose stories and novels examining women's sensuality and desire for independence scandalized the literary establishment of her day.

Just a short distance north on La. 119 stands **Magnolia Plantation Home and Bed and Breakfast** *(5487 La. 119. 318-379-2221. Fee for tours),* the "big house" of a plantation that has remained a working farm in the same family since the original French land grant of 1753. An 1830s house was burned by Union troops retreating after their defeat at the Battle of Mansfield in 1864; the current structure was completed in 1896, using the original brick foundation, walls, and pillars.

Continue north on La. 119 to **Melrose Plantation**★ *(La. 119 and La. 493. 318-379-0055. Adm. fee),* whose history occupies a fascinating niche in Louisiana's cultural mosaic. Born a slave in 1742 in nearby Natchitoches, Marie Thérèse Coincoin was sold to Thomas Pierre Metoyer, who fathered 10 of her 14 children. After being emancipated in the late

18th century, Marie Thérèse and her children obtained land grants and built Yucca Plantation. The original house still stands behind the circa 1833 "big house," built by Marie Thérèse's heirs and enlarged and renamed Melrose by later owners. In the 20th century Melrose became a kind of informal arts colony; William Faulkner and Alexander Woollcott were among those who visited.

The first thing you should know about ❹ **Natchitoches** *(Tourist Commission, Front and Lafayette Sts. 318-352-8072 or 800-259-1714)* is how to pronounce it: "NACK-uh-tish" is close enough to make you understood. The second thing is that the city was established by French traders in 1714, making it the oldest permanent European settlement in the Louisiana Purchase. Natchitoches's historic district along the Cane River includes a section of Front Street with New Orleans-style cast-iron balconies; pick up a walking tour brochure at the Tourist Commission. **Fort St. Jean Baptiste State Commemorative Area** *(133 Moreau St. 318-357-3101 or 888-677-7853. Adm. fee)* is a replica of the 1730s fort, built with local materials using construction methods of the time. The complex includes a chapel, powder magazine, and barracks for the soldiers who were stationed here to prevent Spaniards from making incursions into French territory.

Fort St. Jean Baptiste State Commemorative Area, Natchitoches

Follow La. 1 and La. 7 north to **Minden** *(Tourism Bureau 318-377-4240 or 800-2MINDEN)*, then take Germantown Road 7 miles farther north through rolling pinewoods to ❺ **Germantown Colony and Museum** *(120 Museum Rd. 318-377-6061. March-Nov. Wed.-Sat.; adm. fee)*, site of a German Utopian Movement settlement founded in 1835 and run as a commune until its dissolution in 1871. Three original buildings remain here—two cabins (one of which belonged to the "countess" who led the colony) and a kitchen-dining hall. The smokehouse and blacksmith shop have been reconstructed, and furnishings and artifacts include many items used by the first colonists.

Return to the Shreveport-Bossier City area via I-20.

● 300 miles ● 4 to 5 days ● Year-round, but humidity and mosquitoes can be a trial in midsummer.

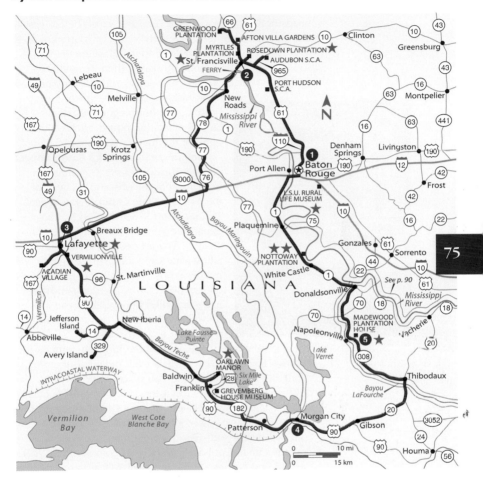

Thanks to dishes like blackened redfish and the danceable beat of chank-a-chank music, people all over the world have at least a nodding acquaintance with the Cajun culture of southern Louisiana. Along with the popularity of their food and music, Cajuns in recent decades have also seen a renaissance of pride in their heritage— a story that begins in loss and exile. In 1755 the British forced the French-speaking people living in eastern Canada (a region then called Acadie or Acadia) to leave their homeland. Eventually a few thousand of these Acadians settled in Louisiana, where for more than two centuries their descendants have held on to their language and customs—although, just as "Acadians" evolved into

"Cajuns," their way of life has been transformed by time and locality into something unique in America.

Beginning in the capital city of Baton Rouge, this drive heads north to historic West Feliciana Parish before crossing the Mississippi River by ferryboat. The route runs west over the vast Atchafalaya Swamp to Lafayette, the self-styled "capital of French Louisiana"; then it's south to sample gardens, elegant old houses, and even a bit of aviation history. The last segment turns north again, finishing at the South's largest plantation house, back on the bank of the muddy Mississippi.

Louisiana Old State Capitol

Get an overview of **❶ Baton Rouge** *(Visitors Bureau 504-383-1825 or 800-LA-ROUGE)* from the observation deck of the 34-story **State Capitol** *(State Capitol Dr. and N. 3rd St. 504-342-7317)*, with expansive views up and down the Mississippi. The art deco-style building, the tallest state capitol in America, was commissioned by Huey P. Long, the legendary politician who ruled Louisiana like a (usually) benevolent dictator until he was fatally shot in one of the hallways here in 1935.

Speaking of the Kingfish, it might be said that Louisiana is to politics what Indiana is to auto racing: It's the big time, and you've got to be awfully quick to survive. Learn about the state's colorful political characters at the castlelike **Louisiana Old State Capitol** *(100 North Blvd. 504-342-0500 or 800-488-2968. Closed Mon.; adm. fee)*, where well-presented exhibits focus on state government and political campaigns. Completed in 1849, the building burned during the Civil War, was reconstructed in 1882, and has been beautifully restored to show off a splendid stained-glass dome, a cast-iron staircase, and all manner of fancy decorative accessories.

Just a block away, the **USS *Kidd* and Nautical Center★** *(305 S. River Rd. 504-342-1942. Adm. fee)* is a fascinating historic site, sure to evoke a rush of memories for World War II veterans. The *Kidd,* a 376-foot-long destroyer that saw much action in the Pacific, now floats in the Mississippi, restored to an almost eerie degree of authenticity: As you walk the halls and climb ladders between the decks, it seems as though the crew has just stepped out for shore leave, with the messroom set for a meal and 1940s pinups on the walls. Military memorabilia in the onshore museum includes a P-40 Flying Tiger World War II fighter and an A-7E Corsair plane from the Vietnam War.

While glorious plantation houses are scattered all along the Mississippi River in Louisiana, the lifestyle they portray represents that of only a tiny percentage of the South's 19th-century rural population. The excellent **L.S.U. Rural Life Museum** ★ *(4600 Essen Ln. at I-10. 504-765-2437. Adm. fee)* addresses that imbalance, giving visitors an idea of how the working class lived in the preindustrial era. The more than 20 buildings on the grounds include slave cabins (rarely preserved anywhere), an 1890 Baptist church (with painted, not stained-glass, windows), an 1863 dogtrot house, and a four-hole outhouse. The museum's main display building contains farm vehicles; tools; and exhibits on old-time medicine, logging, hunting and fishing, and textiles.

Fourteen miles north of Baton Rouge on US 61, **Port Hudson State Commemorative Area** *(504-654-3775 or 888-677-3400. Adm. fee)* preserves the site of some of the bloodiest fighting of the Civil War. Beginning May 23, 1863, Union forces laid siege to Confederate fortifications controlling this strategic location on the Mississippi River.

USS *Kidd* and Nautical Center

Forty-eight days later, news of the Confederate surrender upriver at Vicksburg and a shortage of supplies so severe that men were reduced to eating mules and rats led to the Rebel surrender here. Exhibits in the Interpretive Center describe the ordeal; walking trails wind past earthworks constructed by the defenders.

The pioneering artist and naturalist John James

Grace Episcopal Church and Cemetery, St. Francisville

Audubon spent four months in 1821 near St. Francisville, at Oakley Plantation, tutoring the wealthy owner's young daughter; while here he worked on several paintings for *Birds of America*, including his lively depiction of mockingbirds. The circa 1800 Oakley house is now the centerpiece of the **Audubon State Commemorative Area** *(11788 La. 965. 504-635-3739 or 888-677-2838. Adm. fee).*

❷ **St. Francisville** ★ *(Tourist Commission 504-635-6330)* has a wonderfully diverse history, including a period of 74 days in 1810 when it was the capital of the independent Republic of West Florida. The **West Feliciana Historical Society Museum** *(11757 Ferdinand St. 504-635-6330)* can provide a walking tour guide to the downtown area, which comprises dozens of historically significant buildings.

Scattered through the nearby hills are a number of plantation houses offering tours. **Rosedown Plantation and Historic Gardens** ★ *(12501 La. 10. 504-635-3332. Adm. fee)* was begun in 1835 by wealthy cotton planters Daniel and Martha Turnbull; fronted by an avenue of live oaks, the house is surrounded by 28 acres of gardens. (Avid gardener Martha Turnbull was among the first in the South to plant azaleas.) The house itself is a time capsule: It was occupied by the same family for 120 years and retains its original contents. The most astounding piece of furniture is the 13-foot-tall poster bed in the master bedroom, part of a suite intended for the White House but brought here after Henry Clay's defeat in 1844.

The original section of the **Myrtles Plantation** *(7747 US 61 N. 504-635-6277. Adm. fee)* was built in 1796; much enlarged since then, it now features a 107-foot-long front gallery (porch) with iron grillwork. Though its villa burned in 1963, **Afton Villa Gardens** *(9247 US 61 N. 504-635-6773. March-June and Oct.-Nov.; adm. fee)* still offers fine formal plantings and a winding alley of oaks and azaleas. **Greenwood Plantation** *(6838 Highland Rd., W of US 61. 504-655-4475. Adm. fee)* is a 1980 reconstruction of a magnificent 1830 Greek Revival house that burned in 1960.

From St. Francisville, continue west on La. 10 and cross the Mississsippi River on the ferry *(504-231-4131. Fare)*; La. 10 and La. 1 lead to the 1750 **Parlange Plantation House** *(La. 1, S of New Roads. 504-638-8410. Call for appt.; adm. fee)*. The raised-cottage-style residence here, built of brick and bald cypress, is the "big house" of a working sugar plantation owned by the same family for eight generations, since the original 18th-century French land grant. Then follow La. 78, 77, 76, and 3000 south to I-10, where you'll turn west to cross the broad floodplain of the **Atchafalaya River,** America's largest river-basin swamp. Access to the interior of this wilderness is difficult for the inexperienced, but tour companies in places like Henderson offer boat trips that provide a glimpse of the wildlife and natural beauty here. Call the Lafayette Visitors Commission (see below) for details.

Beyond Bayou Vermilion is ❸ **Lafayette** ★ *(Visitors Commission 318-232-3808 or 800-346-1958)*, where you're definitely in the heart of the Cajun world. To put things into a historical context, visit the **Acadian Cultural Center** *(501 Fisher Rd. 318-232-0789)*, a unit of **Jean Lafitte National Historical Park and Preserve** (which operates several sites in southern Louisiana; see pp. 82, 87, and 89). Here you can watch a well-produced film on *le Grand Dérangement,* as the 18th-century Acadians called their expulsion from Canada; you'll also find exhibits on Cajun life past and present, from architecture to music to foods like *boudin* (spicy pork sausage).

Just next door is **Vermilionville** ★ *(1600 Surrey St. 318-233-4077 or 800-99-BAYOU. Adm. fee)*, a complex of buildings relocated or reconstructed along Bayou Vermilion to portray an early day Acadian village. The sound of fiddle and accordion music floats over the scene from the dance hall, while craftspeople demonstrate their skills in various venues. The oldest building at

Me Oh My, Crawfish Pie

Of all the foods associated with Cajun country, none is more beloved or ubiquitous than the crawfish, that humble crustacean also known as crayfish, crawdad, or mudbug. You'll find it cooked as crawfish *étouffée*—a peppery stew served with rice—or simply boiled, served whole, and eaten with the fingers. (Most restaurants bring you a bib for this slightly messy meal.) How popular is the little critter? Sixty-three million pounds of Louisiana crawdads were sold in a recent year, more than half that amount farm-raised. And that doesn't count the number that folks caught, took home, and popped into the pot themselves.

79

Crawfish feast

Vermilionville is the 1790 Amand Broussard House, an impressively large French Acadian home with walls of *bousillage,* a mixture of mud, Spanish moss, and animal hair.

On the other side of town, but on the same theme, is **Acadian Village** *(200 Greenleaf Dr., off Ridge Rd. 318-981-2364. Adm. fee),* with an interesting collection of restored houses (one dating back to 1800) filled with antiques, tools, and odds and ends. Some are quite rustic, while others reflect a more well-to-do lifestyle. On display is the birthplace of Dudley J. LeBlanc, a politician (and inventor of a "miracle" tonic) whose writings helped spark a rebirth of Cajun pride, after a period early in this century when children were forbidden to speak French in Louisiana schools.

Lafayette (née Vermilionville) was founded in the 1820s on land donated by wealthy plantation owner Jean Mouton. A small house he built in 1800 was enlarged by his son and is now known as the **Alexandre Mouton House, the Lafayette Museum** *(1122 Lafayette St. 318-234-2208. Closed Mon.; adm. fee).* It displays period antiques and personal items of the Mouton family. Jean's grandson, Alfred, was a Confederate general who died at the 1864 Battle of Mansfield in northwestern Louisiana.

Two of the state's most famous Cajun restaurants are found in Lafayette: **Randol's Restaurant and Cajun Dancehall** *(2320 Kaliste Saloom Rd. 318-981-7080)* and **Prejean's** *(3480 US 167 N. 318-896-3247).* Both offer Cajun and seafood dishes and Cajun music and dancing every night. If you'd like more dining suggestions,

Ruins of sugarcane presses near Lafayette

just talk to a local: Nothing gets a conversation going better in Lafayette than asking where you can find the best Cajun food.

Take US 90 south through the sugarcane fields to **New Iberia** *(Tourist Commission 318-365-1540)* and **Shadows-on-the-Teche** *(317 E. Main St. 318-369-6446. Adm. fee),* a dormered and white-columned house on the west bank of Bayou Teche. Built in 1834 by a wealthy cane planter and now operated by the National Trust for Historic

Preservation, the Shadows in its furnishings and family items is a fine depiction of antebellum plantation life in Louisiana. Drive west on La. 14 to **Rip van Winkle Gardens on Jefferson Island** *(5505 Rip van Winkle Rd. 318-365-3332 or 800-375-3332. Adm. fee)*, where 25 acres of continuously blooming gardens surround the ornate Joseph Jefferson House, named for the then famous actor who built it circa 1870. The house still contains items that belonged to Jefferson, including some of the paintings he did to relax between stage appearances.

Southwest of New Iberia, **Avery Island** *(La. 329. Toll)* offers two attractions: The **Jungle Gardens** *(318-369-6243. Adm. fee)* comprise extensive plantings of native and exotic species, along with wildlife including alligators, nutria (a fur-bearing rodent introduced from South America), and, in spring and early summer, thousands of nesting herons and egrets. Visitors may also tour the **McIlhenny Co. factory** *(318-365-8163. Closed Sun.)* to see how the famous Tabasco brand pepper sauce is made.

Follow La. 182 south past Baldwin and turn left to **Oaklawn Manor**★ *(Irish Bend Rd., Franklin. 318-828-0434. Adm. fee)*, a massive and imposing Greek Revival-style house surrounded by huge live oaks and formal gardens. Built in 1837, with handmade brick walls 20 inches thick, Oaklawn is elegantly appointed with marble fireplaces, Baccarat-crystal chandeliers, original paintings by John James Audubon, and hummingbird prints by John Gould. One section of marble floor was moved to the house from a New Orleans hotel destroyed by fire. If the aviary outside looks familiar, you may have seen it in a Paul Newman movie called *The Drowning Pool* (1976), partly filmed here.

As you enter **Franklin** *(Tourism Center 318-828-2555)*, be sure to walk or drive along Main Street to see a fine row of houses from the turn of the century and before. On Sterling Road (La. 322) stands the **Grevemberg House Museum** *(407 Sterling Rd./La. 322. 318-828-2092. Adm. fee)*, an 1851 town house displaying mid-19th-century antiques and local memorabilia.

At Patterson, stop at the **Wedell-Williams Memorial Aviation Museum** *(La. 182. 504-395-7067. Tues.-Sat.; adm. fee)* to learn the remarkable story of Jimmy Wedell, the one-eyed flier who dominated air racing in the early 1930s and was the first pilot to exceed 300 miles per hour; the museum also features a small collection of planes.

In ❹ **Morgan City** *(Tourist Commission 504-395-4905 or 800-256-2931)*, the **Turn-of-the-Century House and Mardi**

Sign for Avery Island's famed pepper sauce

Family Fun

As the New Orleans Mardi Gras has become increasingly, shall we say, R-rated, many people have looked to other towns for less raw and raunchy celebrations of "Fat Tuesday," the traditional period of exuberant eating and drinking before Lent. Lafayette offers a grand parade and a ball open to all, while cities from Houma to Shreveport hold parades, dances, fairs, and parties. In the "prairie" Cajun country around Eunice, some towns still celebrate *le courir de Mardi Gras* (the Mardi Gras run), in which masked riders travel the countryside begging for food and staging ritualized ceremonies. The dates of Mardi Gras vary from year to year, so check with local tourist commissions for details.

81

Lower Atchafalaya Basin along US 90, near Morgan City

Gras Collection *(715 2nd St. 504-380-4651. Closed Mon.; adm. fee)* was built in 1906 of bald cypress timbers salvaged from an earlier residence; its floors are longleaf pine. Period furnishings reflect upper-middle-class life of its time, including a children's room with old games and toys. Upstairs is a display of costumes from local Mardi Gras celebrations.

At Gibson, take La. 20 to **Thibodaux** *(Lafourche Parish Tourist Commission 504-537-5800),* home of the **Wetlands Acadian Cultural Center** *(314 St. Mary St. 504-448-1375),* another unit of **Jean Lafitte National Historical Park and Preserve.** The Thibodaux location focuses on the culture and history of the Cajuns who settled in the swamps and marshes of southern Louisiana, as distinct from the "prairie" Cajuns who live farther northwest (e.g., around Eunice). Located in a grand old building—a warehouse constructed beside Bayou Lafourche circa 1911—the center offers interpretive displays, video presentations, a gallery with changing exhibits, and music shows. Just outside town, **Laurel Valley Village** *(595 La. 308. 504-447-2902. Closed Mon.)* comprises original 19th- and early 20th-century structures of the largest intact sugar plantation in the South. The more than 60 buildings include a general store, 1910 schoolhouse, rustic dwellings, and the remains of a sugar mill.

From Thibodaux, drive north along La. 308 and Bayou Lafourche to ❺ **Madewood Plantation House** ★

(4250 La. 308. 504-369-7151 or 800-375-7151. Adm. fee), the very picture of an Old South mansion, with its six white columns dominating a majestic Greek Revival facade. Madewood was indeed made of wood—cypress trees cut on the property—as well as brick made on the premises; construction began in 1846 and was completed in 1850. The 21-room interior is just as striking as the exterior, with huge cypress pocket doors dividing a double parlor, beautiful woodwork, and a spacious ballroom. Guests can stay overnight in the mansion's antique-filled rooms.

If you were impressed by Madewood, be prepared to be amazed by **Nottoway Plantation**★★ *(La. 1, White Castle. 504-545-2730. Adm. fee)*—all 64 rooms of it. The enormous house was designed by New Orleans architect Henry Howard (who also designed Madewood), and built between 1849 and 1859 for sugar planter John Randolph. The family had 11 children...but even so, 53,000 square feet must have bordered on the excessive. The 7,500-acre plantation had its own plant for producing gas to light the house, which boasted hot water and 16 coal-burning marble fireplaces. The rosewood furniture in the master bedroom was custom-made in New Orleans to fit the space, and many of the other furnishings are original as well. Although Nottoway was shelled during the Civil War, it survived the conflict with little damage; 90 percent of the glass in the house is original. Just to give you an idea of Nottoway's prestige: David O. Selznick wanted to film part of *Gone With the Wind* here—but the owners, not wanting the place cluttered up with Hollywood types, turned him down.

Return to Baton Rouge on La. 1 and I-10.

Sugarcane train engine, Laurel Valley Village

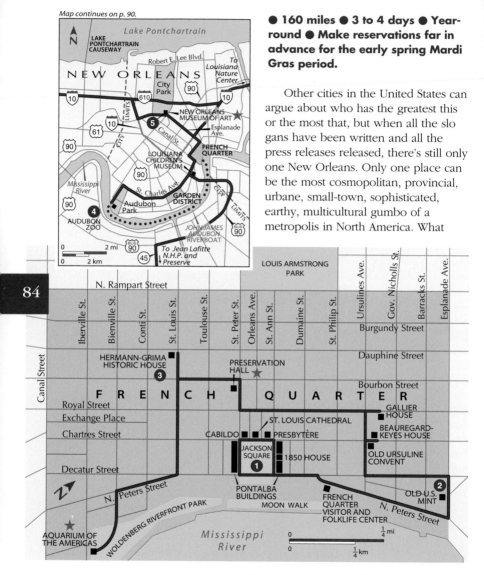

Map continues on p. 90.

● 160 miles ● 3 to 4 days ● Year-round ● Make reservations far in advance for the early spring Mardi Gras period.

Other cities in the United States can argue about who has the greatest this or the most that, but when all the slo gans have been written and all the press releases released, there's still only one New Orleans. Only one place can be the most cosmopolitan, provincial, urbane, small-town, sophisticated, earthy, multicultural gumbo of a metropolis in North America. What

84

other city was christened for a scandalously debauched French duke, promoted by a crooked Scotsman, and governed for a time by a Spaniard named O'Reilly? In New Orleans, the spirit of laid-back hedonism presides over the second busiest port in the country. In New Orleans, people walk around on dry land 6 feet below sea level. In New Orleans, you practically need to learn a second language to get around: *Uptown, downtown, riverside,* and *lakeside* replace the points of the compass, a median is *neutral ground,* and a sidewalk is a *banquette.* And if

In the French Quarter

you think all that's complicated, just try to pin down exactly what *Creole* really means (see sidebar p. 70).

After exploring New Orleans, this drive travels up the Mississippi River to visit a selection of gracious plantation houses—reminders of the vanished Old South, and peaceful counterpoints to the bustle of the city.

Many residents of **New Orleans** ★ ★ *(Visitors Bureau 504-566-5011 or 800-672-6124)* who live uptown (southwest of Canal Street) will quite readily tell you that they never go to the **French Quarter** ★ ★ *(Bordered by Canal, N. Rampart, and Decatur Sts. and Esplanade Ave.),* believing it too commercialized and touristy. Of course, every tourist wants to see the Quarter first...and well they should. Also known by its French name, Vieux Carré (Old Square), this district of fewer than 100 square blocks on the north bank of the Mississippi centers on land where the city was founded in 1718. Today it's a mixed residential and business neighborhood, full of historic buildings, museums, hotels, music clubs, and restaurants of all description. Though the city extends far beyond its boundaries, to millions of people around the world the French Quarter *is* New Orleans.

❶ Jackson Square *(Bordered by St. Peter, Chartres, St. Ann, and Decatur Sts.)* is the place to start your investigation of the Quarter. Originally a French military parade ground called the Place d'Armes, the square was renamed in 1856 for Andrew Jackson, the hero of the 1815 Battle of New Orleans. (His equestrian statue here was the first ever erected with only two of the horse's hooves on the ground.) Across Chartres Street is the grandly towered **St. Louis Cathedral** *(504-525-9585),* the country's oldest active

Touring the French Quarter

cathedral; the building's present appearance dates from 1850.

Flanking the cathedral are two historically significant structures, now locations of the **Louisiana State Museum** *(504-568-6968 or 800-568-6968. Closed Mon.; adm. fee).* The **Cabildo,** dating from about 1795, served as a government building throughout early New Orleans history. The 1803 ceremony transferring the vast territory of the Louisiana Purchase from France to the United States took place in a second-floor room here. Museum exhibits trace the history of Louisiana and include a death mask of Napoleon Bonaparte (who sold all that land to the U.S.). On the other side of the cathedral, the **Presbytère** was begun in the 1790s as a residence for parish priests (though none ever lived here) and now displays varied artifacts from Louisiana's past as well as changing exhibits.

As you look out from the cathedral, the twin structures on the left and right of the square are the **Pontalba Buildings,** completed in 1850 by the wealthy Baroness

86

Mardi Gras bustle on Bourbon Street

Pontalba as luxury apartments and shops. You'll find another location of the Louisiana State Museum, the **1850 House** *(523 St. Ann St. 504-568-6968. Closed Mon.; adm. fee)*, in the "lower" Pontalba Building; its rooms are furnished with authentic items from the mid-19th century, re-creating a middle-class New Orleans residence of the antebellum years. A **Tourist Information Center** *(529 St. Ann St. 504-568-5661)* offering advice about both New Orleans and Louisiana is located nearby.

Across Decatur Street stands a 24-hour restaurant that's become a true institution of the Quarter. **Café du Monde** *(800 Decatur St. 504-581-2914)* is famed for café au lait (coffee with milk) and beignets (something like a square doughnut coated with powdered sugar). If you keep going toward the Mississippi you'll find the **Moon Walk** (named for former Mayor Moon Landrieu), a riverside promenade where you can watch huge tankers and cargo ships passing by.

Jean Lafitte National Historical Park and Preserve encompasses several locations across southern Louisiana. Among them, the **French Quarter Visitor and Folklife Center** *(916 N. Peters St. 504-589-2636)* presents exhibits and programs on regional culture and history, and

rangers lead daily walks through both the Quarter and the uptown Garden District (see sidebar p. 88); check at the Visitor Center for schedules. Continuing downriver past the **French Market,** an area of shops and restaurants that also includes a Farmers' Market, you'll come to the ❷ **Old U.S. Mint** *(400 Esplanade Ave. 504-568-6968. Closed Mon.; adm. fee)*, another part of the Louisiana State Museum. This 1835 building, which at various times in its past turned out both U.S. and Confederate money, now houses exhibits on jazz and Mardi Gras.

Fires in 1788 and 1794 destroyed most of the original French Quarter; one edifice that survived was the 1734 **Old Ursuline Convent** *(1100 Chartres St. 504-529-3040. Closed Mon.; adm. fee)*. Once the home of the Sisters of St. Ursula, French nuns who came to New Orleans in 1727 to establish a school, the convent now offers tours of its beautifully restored building. Two nearby historic residences are also open

Old Man River's Wayward Ways

The path the Mississippi River takes on its final run to the Gulf of Mexico is in no way a permanent feature of the landscape. The river has changed course many times in the latest geological era: on average, perhaps once every thousand years. Both Bayou Teche and Bayou Lafourche have (relatively) recently been the "main" Mississippi—and, were it not for control structures maintained by the U.S. Army Corps of Engineers, the river's primary flow would almost certainly already have moved into the Atchafalaya far upstream from New Orleans. The consequences of such an event are formidable, since shipping could be cut off from a heavily industrialized stretch of the river, and New Orleans, the country's second busiest port, could be left a backwater. Human ingenuity has solved many problems, but there are those who believe that, despite our best efforts, in time the Mighty Mississippi will go where it wants to go.

87

Garden District

Shunned by the aristocratic French Creoles, the Yankees who flocked to New Orleans following the 1803 Louisiana Purchase built their lavish mansions outside the French Quarter, on the southwest side of Canal Street (uptown). Resplendent with predominately Greek Revival architecture and punctuated by fountains, statuary, and gardens galore, the neighborhood became known as the Garden District. For a peek at the belle epoque of the early 19th century, Prytania Street is a fine place to begin a stroll. The circa 1838 **Toby's Corner** *(2340 Prytania St.)* is a raised cottage thought to be the district's oldest home; the nearby 1850 **Payne-Strachan House** *(1134 1st St.)* is where Confederate President Jefferson Davis died while visiting in 1889. And don't miss **Lafayette Cemetery Number 1** *(1428 Washington Ave.)*, one of New Orleans's fabled above ground "cities of the dead."

to visitors: The 1826 **Beauregard-Keyes House** *(1113 Chartres St. 504-523-7257. Closed Sun.; adm. fee)* was home to Confederate Gen. P.G.T. Beauregard and novelist Frances Parkinson Keyes; the **Gallier House** *(1118-1132 Royal St. 504-525-5661. Closed Sun.; adm. fee)*, completed in 1860, was built by James Gallier, Jr., a well-known New Orleans architect, and is furnished in the style of the city's well-to-do in the mid-19th century.

Music is everywhere in the French Quarter, but the most famous venue is undoubtedly **Preservation Hall** ★ *(726 St. Peter St. 504-522-2841. Nightly at 8:00; adm. fee)*, where people go to hear traditional jazz played enthusiastically but respectfully—not to eat or drink or talk, but just to listen. The list of famous New Orleans musicians is long and eclectic, and bars and clubs are abundant, so check local publications to see who might be appearing around town during your visit. A bit farther away, the 1831 ❸ **Hermann-Grima Historic House** *(820 St. Louis St. 504-525-5661. Closed Sun.; adm. fee)* features a stately interior, a formal courtyard garden, and a historically important kitchen and stable.

Moving to the outskirts of the Quarter now, the **Aquarium of the Americas** ★ *(1 Canal St. 504-581-4629 or 800-774-7394. Adm. fee)* is one of the city's must-see attractions. Showcasing North and South American species, the aquarium includes a 400,000-gallon Gulf of Mexico exhibit and displays on Caribbean reefs and the Amazon River. The creatures you'll see here range from alligators and sea turtles to sharks and jellyfish. Southwest of the Quarter, the **Louisiana Children's Museum** *(420 Julia St. 504-523-1357. Closed Mon.; adm. fee)* offers a broad array of activities, from exhibits on physics and physical fitness to areas where kids can pretend to be TV stars or tugboat captains. The fine ❹ **Audubon Zoo** *(6500 Magazine St. in Audubon Park. 504-861-2537 or 800-774-7394. Adm. fee)* is another treat for animal lovers, with its famed white alligators in the Louisiana Swamp exhibit.

French Quarter banjo player

An excellent way to see the aquarium, children's museum, and zoo is to ride the historic **St. Charles Streetcar Line** *(504-248-3900. Fare)* from Canal Street past the fine old houses of the Garden District to the zoo, and then take the *John James*

Audubon riverboat *(504-586-8777. Fare)* back to the aquarium.

To the north, in City Park, the ❺ **New Orleans Museum of Art**★ *(1 Collins Diboll Cir. 504-488-2631. Closed Mon.; adm. fee)* is known for its collections of French and American art, Japanese paintings, and African art, as well as one of the South's finest decorative art collections, including three of Peter Carl Fabergé's famed Russian Imperial Easter eggs.

Fish-watching at the Aquarium of the Americas

Two sites not far from the city center offer good introductions to the natural environment of southern Louisiana. Nature trails wind through 86 acres of woods and wetlands at the **Louisiana Nature Center** *(Off Read Blvd. in Joe W. Brown Memorial Park. 504-246-5672. Closed Mon.; adm. fee)*, and a planetarium offers changing shows on astronomy. To the south of New Orleans, the **Barataria Preserve Unit** *(7400 La. 45, Marrero. 504-589-2330)* of **Jean Lafitte National Historical Park and Preserve** encompasses some 20,000 acres of varied habitat, from the forests that grow on slightly elevated natural levees down to lower-lying marshland. Hiking and canoe trails allow exploration of the preserve, providing close looks at alligators, nutria, wading birds, songbirds, and other wildlife.

The rich bottomland soil of the Mississippi Delta, along with the labor of slaves, became the foundation on which huge fortunes were built in the early 19th century, when farmers established expansive sugarcane plantations along the riverbank and throughout the surrounding countryside. Louisiana is said to have been the second richest state in America before the Civil War, and plantation owners vied with each other to build the finest mansions with the costliest furnishings. Many houses were destroyed in the war (and many fortunes were lost), but a few survived and have been restored to their antebellum glory. A drive up the north bank of the Mississippi and down the south will take you to some of these historic houses. To begin, return to Business US 90, go west to I-310, north across the river to La. 48 (River Road), and turn right.

❻ **Destrehan Plantation** *(13034 River Rd./La. 48. 504 764-9315. Adm. fee)* stands as the oldest documented plantation house in the lower Mississippi Valley.

89

Originally built in 1787 with hand-hewn bald cypress timber and *bousillage* (mud, Spanish moss, and animal hair) walls, it was expanded and remodeled in the 19th century to its present appearance, a blend of traditional West Indies and Greek Revival styles. Wide galleries provide shade, and large doors and windows catch any breeze. Destrehan began as an indigo plantation, but later switched to sugarcane when the latter crop's superiority caused a boom in plantings in the early 1800s.

Proceed upstream on the River Road, which eventually is called La. 44 and takes you to **San Francisco Plantation**★ *(504-535-2341. Adm. fee),* an 1856 home whose name is as interesting as its architecture is eclectic. Because the house was so expensive, its first owner called it St. Frusquin, a bit of wordplay on the French phrase *sans fruscins*—"without a penny"; a later owner changed it to the more genteel San Francisco. The highly decorated steamboat Gothic exterior is flanked by large cisterns; the wonderfully restored (and, in places like the Lady's Parlor, amazingly colorful) interior features elaborate ceiling murals and sumptuous furnishings.

Farther west on La. 44, beyond the tall Sunshine Bridge, **Tezcuco Plantation Home** *(3158 La. 44. 504-562-3929. Adm. fee)* is at the center of a complex of bed-and-breakfast cabins, shops, and outbuildings. Its Greek Revival-style exterior is more modest than that of many plantation mansions; its interior includes fine plasterwork, false-grained wood, and period antiques. Construction began in 1855 and lasted five years, making Tezcuco one of the last of the grand homes completed before the Civil War. Also on the grounds is the **River Road African American Museum and Gallery** *(504-644-7955. Call for appt.; adm. fee),* with artifacts of the slavery era.

Take La. 942 to ❼ **Houmas House Plantation and Gardens** *(504-473-7841. Adm. fee),* the "big house" of what was once Louisiana's largest sugarcane plantation. (The house and surrounding 12,000 acres sold for one million dollars in 1858, and plantings later grew to 20,000 acres.) With its stately white columns and gardens, Houmas House recalls a patrician world of privilege and wealth.

Return to the Sunshine Bridge, cross the Mississippi, and turn left on La. 18 to reach one of the most photographed scenes in Louisiana: the quarter-mile-long double row of live oaks fronting **Oak Alley Plantation**  *(3645 La. 18. 504-265-2151 or 800-442-5539. Adm. fee).* These gnarled limbs have seen a lot of history since they were planted by an unknown French settler in the early 18th century; they've long since grown together to form a green tunnel leading from the house toward the river. The Greek Revival mansion, with its 28 massive brick columns, was built in the late 1830s; its interior has been carefully and elegantly restored.

Continue 3 miles on La. 18 to **Laura: A Creole Plantation** *(La. 18. 504-265-7690. Adm. fee).* Rather than a mansion tour, this site offers an entire Creole plantation complex, including an 1805 manor house, 1840s slave cabins, and bald cypress Creole cottages (1820-1880s). Based in part on the memoirs of Laura Locoul, who was born here in 1861, the tours emphasize the daily lives of owners and slaves, men, women, and children.

Return to New Orleans on La. 18, I-310, and I-10.

91

Oak Alley Plantation, built in the 1830s

Gulf Coast

● **140 miles** ● **3 to 4 days** ● **Year-round** ● **US 90 around Gulfport and Biloxi can be very congested in summer.**

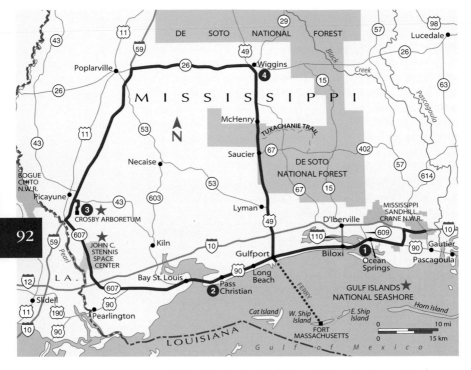

The Mississippi Gulf Coast? Keep looking…It's there, all right, in among the mammoth casinos that have sprouted along the once tranquil shoreline like neon-lit mushrooms. Gambling is big business in Mississippi these days, and nowhere has the effect been greater than in the coast towns from Biloxi to Bay St. Louis—which, if not yet rivaling Las Vegas, at least provide a pretty good simulation. If you enjoy the nonstop action and 50-item buffet lines of casinos, this is good news. If not, don't worry: History, nature, art, and the laid-back beach life still exist, and this drive samples a little of all of them.

You begin in Ocean Springs, a haven of tranquility across the Biloxi Bay Bridge from the casino lights, and then head west on US 90; old and new meet here, with gracious houses and museums cheek by jowl with high-rise hotels. After a short trip out of this world (at the Stennis Space Center), you'll turn inland to see more of the natural side of the Magnolia State. For information on all coast attractions, call the **Mississippi Gulf Coast Convention & Visitors Bureau** (*228-896-6699 or 888-467-4853*).

In **❶ Ocean Springs** *(Chamber of Commerce 228-875-4424)*, **Walter Anderson Museum of Art** *(510 Washington Ave. 228-872-3164. Adm. fee)* is dedicated to an eccentric New Orleans-born artist who produced vibrant, dramatic works depicting the natural environment of the Mississippi coast. In his later years Anderson turned away from "the sort of thing most people call reality," often spending weeks alone on Horn Island, painting birds, shells, and plants. The gallery offers an excellent film on Anderson's life; the adjoining city Community Center contains large murals he painted in 1950-51. Other members of the Anderson family founded and still operate **Shearwater Pottery** *(102 Shearwater Dr. 228 875 7320)*, famed for elegant design.

Ocean Springs is home to the Mississippi headquarters of **Gulf Islands National Seashore** ★ *(3500 Park Rd. 228-875-9057)*, which encompasses barrier islands from Gulfport to Fort Walton Beach, Florida. In Mississippi, the seashore includes Petit Bois, Horn, and East Ship Islands—all primitive areas for which visitors must arrange their own transportation and supplies—and West Ship Island, accessible from Gulfport by commercial tour boat (see p. 95). On the mainland at Ocean Springs, the seashore headquarters area offers camping, picnicking, a nature trail, and a Visitor Center with exhibits.

Northeast of town, the **Mississippi Sandhill Crane National Wildlife Refuge** *(Gautier exit off I-10. 228-497-6322.*

Exploring Davis Bayou, part of Gulf Islands National Seashore

Fort Massachusetts, West Ship Island

Mon.-Fri.) protects the breeding habitat for an endangered subspecies of the sandhill crane. Visitors aren't guaranteed a look at the birds, since their nesting areas are off-limits, but staff members give tours to see them in winter (call for reservations). The Visitor Center has exhibits on the cranes, as well as maps to a nature trail through savanna and wetland areas where carnivorous pitcher plants grow.

Biloxi *(Visitor Center, 710 Beach Blvd. 228-374-3105 or 800-245-6943)* was named for a local Indian tribe; in the first decades of this century it was the world's leading seafood producer. The **Maritime and Seafood Industry Museum** *(115 1st St. 228-435-6320. Closed Sun.; adm. fee),* located in a converted Coast Guard station, tells the story of the fishing boats and canneries that once dominated the coast. The locally renowned Biloxi schooner was a special two-masted sailboat developed here for oystering. Built around the turn of the century, the *Glenn L. Swetman* and the *Mike Sekul* offer short cruises along the coast; check at the museum for details. The museum's exhibits and audiovisual presentations on hurricanes, especially 1969's Camille, will surely make you more conscious of the danger of these terrible storms.

Across US 90, the **J.L. Scott Marine Education Center** *(115 Beach Blvd. 228-374-5550. Closed Sun.; adm. fee)* centers on one giant aquarium, and many smaller ones, full of varied sea life from sharks and groupers to crabs and clams—including some types (e.g. red snapper, redfish, flounder) that might end up on your plate while you're visiting the coast. Farther west, beautifully restored 1856 **Tullis-Toledano Manor** *(360 Beach Blvd. 228-435-6293. Mon.-Fri.; adm. fee)* was the home of cotton broker Christoval Toledano; its graceful design features outdoor stairways and ornate dormers. The **Biloxi Mardi Gras Museum** *(119 Magnolia Ave. 228-435-6245. Closed Sun.; adm. fee)* displays elaborate and colorful costumes from past "Fat Tuesday" celebrations. (A walking tour guide to other historic downtown buildings is available from the city Visitor Center.)

Bear in mind, as you cruise the oceanfront strip through Biloxi, that on your left is the largest man-made beach in the world: 26 miles of sand regularly renewed by being dredged up from offshore and dumped back on land. Dead ahead, you can hardly miss the 1848 **Biloxi Lighthouse** *(228-435-6293. Tours by appt.)*, a 65-foot cast-iron landmark situated right in the middle of US 90. Watch, too, for special beach areas set aside in spring and summer to protect nesting areas of the threatened least tern, a small, graceful white bird with a jet-black cap.

In **Gulfport,** catch the 12-mile, hour-long boat ride *(Gulfport Small Craft Harbor, US 90 and US 49. 228-864-1014. March-Oct.; fare)* to **West Ship Island,** and watch for bottlenose dolphins along the way. Once on the island, be sure to visit massive **Fort Massachusetts,** which dates from 1859; park rangers lead tours in summer. A boardwalk traverses the island to the popular swimming beach on the south shore, or you can head out on your own to the eastern end, where you'll find more solitude and, likely, more wildlife. If you go into the water, watch out for jellyfish and stingrays (shuffling your feet while you wade will help protect against the latter).

After a decade of travail and travel following the Civil War, former Confederate President Jefferson Davis retired in 1877 to **Beauvoir** *(2244 Beach Blvd. 228-388-1313. Adm. fee)* to write his memoirs. Today the residence, built in 1853, still contains Davis family furnishings and personal items; the raised American cottage-style house boasts expansive verandas and 14-foot ceilings. A nearby museum displays Civil War artifacts and shows a film on Davis's life; elsewhere on the 50-acre estate are nature trails and the Tomb of the Unknown Confederate Soldier.

Like Ocean Springs, ❷ **Pass Christian** *(Chamber of Commerce 228-452-2252)* (say Chris-CHAN) is a quiet retreat from the glitter of the Biloxi-Gulfport casino strip. Wealthy

When France decided to colonize the vast Mississippi River Valley, claimed for it in 1682 by La Salle, a 1699 exploratory party chose as its first settlement a spot on Biloxi Bay that's now the city of Ocean Springs. Poor soil and constant sickness plagued the tiny colony, here and after it shifted across the bay to present-day Biloxi; after a short period at Mobile, the capital of French Louisiana eventually moved to New Orleans, and Biloxi Bay sank for a time into what one historian called "deserved oblivion." Nonetheless, the French Catholic influence has remained strong along the Mississippi Gulf Coast, with mostly Protestant upstate residents often looking on towns like Bay St. Louis and Biloxi as havens of drinking, gambling, and just generally too much *joie de vivre*—more like decadent New Orleans than like the rest of Mississippi.

95

Jefferson Davis's Beauvoir, Biloxi

plantation owners and businesspeople from New Orleans built second homes here as far back as the early 19th century; the town's yacht club, founded in 1849, is the second oldest in the country. Turn off US 90 onto **Scenic Drive** to see a long line of elegant, 19th-century private houses; rejoin US 90 by turning left at Market Street.

Take Miss. 607 east and north to the **John C. Stennis Space Center**★ *(228-688-2370),* the facility where NASA tests engines for the space shuttle and other rockets. Despite the high-tech and experimental activities taking place here, the center welcomes visitors; you'll even be allowed to watch an engine test if one is scheduled while you're on the grounds. Tours of the complex are given daily, and exhibits in or around the Visitor Center include space suits, models of the space shuttle, interactive displays on space science, and full-size rockets. The Hall of Achievement examines the history and future of space travel.

Continue north now on I-59 toward Picayune and briefly east on Miss. 43 to the ❸ **Crosby Arboretum**★ *(370 Ridge Rd. 601-799-2311. Wed.-Sun.; adm. fee),* an excellent botanical garden focusing on the plants of the Pearl River Basin of southern Mississippi and southeastern Louisiana. At the arboretum's Visitor Center, more than 3 miles of trails wind through wetland and woodland areas where a wide variety of native species grow; interpretive exhibits explain how natural processes including flood and fire help determine the plants found in a particular area. The Crosby manages several diverse areas nearby, including bogs and pine savannas, and offers tours and programs throughout the year; call to find out what's scheduled around the time of your visit.

Rejoin I-59 north to Miss. 26, and go east to ❹ **Wiggins.** At the **De Soto National Forest Ranger Station** *(Miss. 26 at US 49. 601-928-4422. Mon.-Fri.)* here, you can pick up maps and information on camping, hiking, and canoeing. Adventurous travelers might want to float a stretch of Black Creek, a national wild and scenic river, or hike through the Black Creek Wilderness Area. For a quick sampling of the environment here, go south on US 49 past McHenry to the **Tuxachanie Trail.** The first 5 miles of the 22-mile trail are a flat, easy walk along an abandoned railroad bed through a swampy area with abundant birdlife and varied plant species. It makes a fine break from the road, and you can hike as much or as little of it as you have time or energy for.

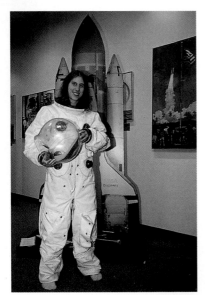

Tourist at John C. Stennis Space Center

Jackson to Natchez ★

● **150 miles** ● **3 to 4 days** ● **Year-round** ● **Azaleas, dogwoods, magnolias, and other blooms brighten spring, but rain is less likely in fall.**

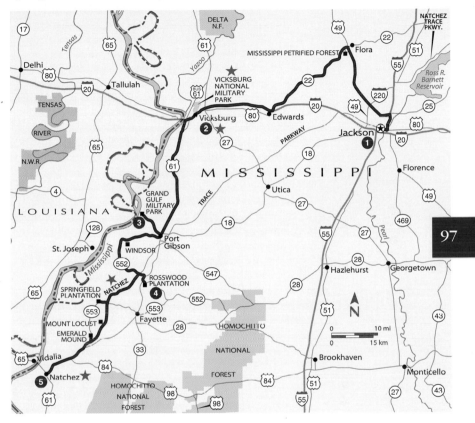

Jackson, Vicksburg, and Natchez—these are names at the very heart of the Old South, evoking memories that shape the image of an entire region. Jackson is the capital of Mississippi, land of magnolia blossoms and cotton farms, where field hands first sang the blues and civil rights supporters fought so many important battles. Vicksburg, blessed and cursed with a strategic location on the Mississippi River, fell to Union forces after a bitter 47-day siege in one of the Civil War's most decisive moments. Natchez, full of elegant and historic houses, remains a living museum of the antebellum years, a bittersweet, romantic time when great fortunes were made and a privileged few lived lives of elegance and refinement.

There's plenty of history along this drive (part of it more than 30 million years old), but before heading west and south to the great battlefield of Vicksburg and the mansions of Natchez, the route begins in the modern city of ❶ **Jackson** *(Visitors Bureau 601-960-1891 or 800-354-7695)*, founded in 1821 on a bluff overlooking the Pearl River and named for "Old Hickory" Andrew Jackson, who just a few years before had defeated the Creek Nation and sent the British running at the Battle of New Orleans.

Learn about the history of Jackson and Mississippi at the **Old Capitol Museum** *(100 S. State St. 601-359-6920)*, one of several fine attractions located in the central city area. Completed in 1838, this columned Greek Revival structure with a 120-foot-tall rotunda served as capitol until the present statehouse was built in 1903. Exhibits examine the influence and interaction of Native American, European, and African-American cultures in Mississippi; a special area looks at the civil rights struggles of 1954-1970, with photographs, posters, and video presentations.

On the other side of the block, the **Mississippi Museum of Natural Science** *(111 N. Jefferson St. 601-354-7303. Closed Sun.; donation)* provides a fine introduction to the state's natural habitats, with displays and dioramas on cypress swamps, Gulf Coast marshes, longleaf pine forests, and bottomland hardwoods, among other environments. If you've never seen a gar or a sunfish (or a catfish that wasn't breaded and fried), you'll find them and many other species in the museum's aquariums.

A few blocks north, **The Oaks House Museum** *(823 N. Jefferson St. 601-353-9339. Tues.-Sat.; adm. fee)* offers a look back to Jackson's antebellum years. Built in the 1850s, this simple Greek Revival cottage survived the Civil War (it was occupied for a time by Gen. William T. Sherman) and the years since with minimal changes. The interior is furnished in a style befitting the family of the original owner, James H. Boyd, a successful businessman and mayor of the city. The **Smith Robertson Museum and Cultural Center** *(528 Bloom St. 601-960-1457. Adm. fee)* is dedicated to African-American history and heritage in Mississippi, with artworks, artifacts, and personal items telling a story of struggle and success. The museum is named for a former slave who went on to become a Jackson alderman in the late 19th century, and who helped establish the city's first school for black children—in the building that now houses the museum. The **Manship House Museum** *(420 E. Fortification St. 601-961-4724. Tues.-Sat.; donation)* is an 1857 Gothic Revival home restored to reflect middle-class life in 1888; inside are examples of Charles Manship's own decorative designs.

North of downtown, the **Mississippi Agriculture and Forestry/National Agriculture Aviation Museum** *(1150*

Front porch at Mississippi Agriculture and Forestry/National Agriculture Aviation Museum

Lakeland Dr. 601-354-6113 or 800-844-8687. Adm. fee) contains an abundance of things to see and do within its complex of historical buildings and museums. The state's farming and forestry industries are saluted in the Heritage Center, which includes displays on crop dusting's pioneers and present-day fliers. Nearby, the Fortenberry-Parkman Farm presents a collection of 19th-century buildings moved from a site in the southern part of the state and restored; the farmstead includes a main house, barns, corn cribs, and a chicken house. "Small Town, Mississippi," comprises a blacksmith shop, schoolhouse, cotton gin, and other buildings typical of a country village.

Near Flora, northwest of Jackson, **Mississippi Petrified Forest** *(Off US 49. 601-879-8189. Adm. fee)* is well worth a detour on the way to Vicksburg. A short trail leads past petrified trees estimated to have lived 36 million years ago; the logs were carried to this site as driftwood by a prehistoric river, buried in sand and silt, and turned to stone as minerals slowly replaced organic matter. Broken and jumbled, the logs (many of them quite large) have been exposed as the soft overlying loess—a fine, wind-deposited soil—has eroded away.

Take Miss. 22 to I-20 and proceed west to ❷ **Vicksburg**★ *(Visitors Bureau 601-636-9421 or 800-221-3536).* Situated at the confluence of the Yazoo and Mississippi Rivers, on an important railway line, the city was described by Abraham Lincoln as the "key" to Union victory in the Civil War. Gen. Ulysses S. Grant's efforts to capture Vicksburg—thus controlling the Mississippi and splitting the Confederacy in half—culminated in one of the war's most harrowing periods: a 47-day siege during which residents lived in hand-dug caves to escape shelling and ran so low on food that "pussy must look out for her safety," as a newspaper of the day reported. Vicksburg fell on July 4, 1863, when Lt. Gen. John C. Pemberton surrendered his troops to Grant.

Memories of the campaign live on at **Vicksburg National Military Park** ★ *(3201 Clay St., just off I-20. 601-636-0583. Adm. fee),* which preserves 1,752 acres where much of the fighting took place. A video presentation in the Visitor Center tells the story of Grant's push toward Vicksburg; exhibits re-create soldiers' quarters and a typical resident's cave shelter. (Thanks to the caves, relatively few civilians were killed during the siege bombardment.) A 16-mile tour route leads past significant battle sites, including the **Shirley House,** the only surviving structure from the siege, and **Fort Garrott,** where Confederate Col. Isham W. Garrott was killed by a Union sharpshooter.

Vicksburg National Military Park

The remains of the USS *Cairo,* a Union ironclad gunboat sunk by a mine on December 12, 1862, are preserved at one stop; a nearby museum displays artifacts recovered from the craft. Audiotapes describing the tour can be rented at the Visitor Center, or you can hire a licensed park guide for a personalized presentation.

After their victory, Union troops triumphantly raised their flag over the grandly columned county courthouse, which they had long viewed in the distance atop one of the city's highest hills. (Confederate officials prevented shelling of the prominent structure by keeping Federal prisoners in the courtroom.) The 1858 building is now the **Old Court House Museum** *(1008 Cherry St. 601-636-0741. Adm. fee),* full of historic items including, of course, many from the wartime period. After the war, the upstairs courtroom was the scene of a trial in which former Confederate President Jefferson Davis sued to regain a nearby plantation that had been confiscated by the U.S. government. The museum showcases Davis's favorite rocking chair and his silver service, as well as artifacts ranging from weapons to jewelry to an 1870 tricycle that looks as if it could severely test the endurance of anyone riding it.

Several of Vicksburg's many historic houses are open as bed-and-breakfast inns, for tours, or both. **Balfour**

House ★ *(1002 Crawford St. 601-638-7113. Closed Sun.; adm. fee)*, a Greek Revival mansion built in 1835, was headquarters for Union Gen. James B. McPherson after the Rebel surrender; it features a graceful spiral staircase and some original furnishings. The **Martha Vick House** *(1300 Grove St. 601-638-7036. Adm. fee)* was built in 1830 for a daughter of Newitt Vick, the Methodist minister for whom the city is named. Among the other notable houses:

Old Court House Museum, Vicksburg

McRaven *(1445 Harrison St. 601-636-1663. March-Nov.; adm. fee)*, built in 1797; **Cedar Grove** *(2300 Washington St. 601-636-1000. Adm. fee)*, an 1840 Greek Revival house with formal gardens and a Union cannonball in the parlor wall; and the **Duff Green Mansion** *(1114 1st East St. 601-636-6968. Adm. fee)*, constructed about 1856 in the Palladian style and used as a hospital by both Union and Confederate troops.

South of Vicksburg on US 61, **Port Gibson** *(Chamber of Commerce, US 61. 601-437-4351)* encompasses a number of historic sites, with additional points of interest just a few miles from town. Stop at the Chamber of Commerce for a driving tour pamphlet to the area; the office is located in the circa 1805 **Samuel Gibson House,** the second home of the town's founder, moved here from its original location and renovated. Port Gibson's most celebrated building is undoubtedly the **First Presbyterian Church** *(US 61 and Walnut St. 601-437-5428)*, where the steeple is topped with a 12-foot-tall gilded hand, its index finger pointed toward heaven; chandeliers in the church came from the steamboat *Robert E. Lee.* Some of the soldiers who died in the May 1, 1863 Battle of Port Gibson, an important part of Grant's march toward Vicksburg, are buried in **Wintergreen Cemetery** *(E end of Greenwood St. 601-439-4351)*, where Confederate Gen. Earl Van Dorn also lies— facing south.

Sign for historic McRaven

❸ **Grand Gulf Military Park** *(Grand Gulf Rd. 601-437-5911. Adm. fee)*, 7 miles northwest of Port Gibson, marks the site of a battle in which Confederate forces turned back Union troops who hoped to begin their push toward Vicksburg. The park includes a museum,

Relaxing at Rosswood Plantation

observation tower, and several restored buildings.

One of the most famous and photographed sites near Port Gibson is a grouping of 23 brick Corinthian columns standing silently in a field 12 miles southwest of town on Miss. 552. The ruins of **Windsor** are all that remain of what was the largest antebellum mansion in Mississippi, completed in 1861 at the then enormous cost of $175,000. The house survived the Civil War—its cupola was used as a lookout by Confederates and it later served as a hospital for Union soldiers—only to burn down in 1890 when a party guest threw a cigarette into construction debris. Nearby, **Canemount Plantation** *(Miss. 552. 601-877-3784 or 800-423-0684)*, a private bed-and-breakfast inn, is a fine example of Italianate Revival architecture. Follow Miss. 552 across US 61 to ❹ **Rosswood Plantation** *(601-437-4215. March-Dec.; adm. fee)*, an 1857 Greek Revival mansion designed by David Shroder, the architect who fashioned Windsor. On display at Rosswood is the journal of the original owner, Dr. Walter Wade, giving a personal account of plantation life and events of the Civil War.

Retrace your path and turn southward on the **Natchez Trace Parkway**★ *(Headquarters 601-680-4025)*, a route administered by the National Park Service that runs more than 400 miles from Natchez to Nashville, Tennessee (see Hills and Delta drive, p. 105). Turn off the parkway at Miss. 553 and drive west a short distance to **Springfield Plantation** *(601-786-3802. Adm. fee)*, built in 1786 and noted for fine woodwork and furnishings.

Travelers on the old Natchez Trace often spent the night at rustic inns called stands; the last surviving original stand on today's parkway is **Mount Locust** *(Milepost 15.5. 601-445-4211)*, now restored to its appearance of the

Mississippi River Bridge, Natchez

1820s, with rail fences and seasonal living history demonstrations of frontier crafts. A little farther south, **Emerald Mound** *(Mile 10.3. 601-680-4025)* is the second largest Native American ceremonial mound in the U.S. Covering 8 acres, the mound was built around A.D. 1250 by Mississippian Indians believed to have been the ancestors of the historic-period Natchez tribe.

It was that latter group, of course, for whom the city of ❺ **Natchez** ★ *(Visitors Bureau, 422 Main St. 601-446-6345 or 800-647-6724)* was named, though they were defeated and scattered in 1729 after conflicts with European settlers. Once the most important Mississippi River port between the Ohio River and New Orleans, antebellum Natchez became wealthy on the cotton trade; an oft-repeated local assertion is that at one time half the millionaires in the United States lived (or at least had houses) in the city. A place of such importance was a top priority for Union forces in the Civil War; they occupied Natchez early, sparing it serious damage. The result is that the city now offers visitors a wealth of history, with more than 300 antebellum buildings scattered in town and nearby.

Before getting to the famous 19th-century mansions, you might begin your explorations even farther back in the past at the **Grand Village of the Natchez Indians** *(400 Jefferson Davis Blvd. 601-446-6502)*. Visitors can walk among ceremonial mounds occupied by the Natchez until their defeat in 1729; a museum displays artifacts of these sun-worshiping Native Americans.

Natchez National Historical Park *(504 S. Canal St. 601-442-7047. Mon.-Fri.)*, a unit of the National Park Service, administers **Melrose Estate** *(1 Melrose-Montebello Pkwy. 601-446-5790. Adm. fee)*, at the center of which is an 1847

Pausing at Stanton Hall, one of Natchez's many antebellum mansions

Greek Revival-Georgian mansion built by a lawyer who also owned extensive cotton lands. Near the house are beautiful formal gardens, and on the grounds stand a carriage house, stable, slave quarters, and other outbuildings. The park is restoring the 1841 **William Johnson House** (210 State St.), the home of a freed slave who became a barber and successful businessman in Natchez. The house will include exhibits on African-American life in early Natchez and on Johnson, who kept a meticulous diary of his life that also serves as a history of the pre-Civil War city. The **Museum of African-American History and Culture** (307A Market St. 601-445-0728. Closed Sun.; adm. fee) features local items and documents, with special focus on the slavery era.

The best way to arrange visits to Natchez tour houses is to stop by the office of **Natchez Pilgrimage Tours** (Canal St. Depot, 200 State St. 601-446-6631 or 800-647-6742) and buy tickets for the places you'd like to see. (The per-house price goes down as you add stops.) The office can also provide a map and advice about the many historic houses that serve as bed-and-breakfasts.

For many visitors, the most extraordinary house in Natchez is **Longwood**★ (140 Lower Woodville Rd. 601-442-5193. Adm. fee), despite the fact that its interior is mostly empty and unfinished. Construction began on this enormous octagonal brick house in 1859, but stopped as the Civil War began in 1861, with only the exterior and one inside level completed. Today it sits like a gigantic red-and-white cake topped with an onion dome, looking as exotic to modern eyes as it must have in the mid-19th century.

Among the more than a dozen other houses open year-round for tours: **Stanton Hall**★ (401 High St. 601-442-6282 or 800-647-6742. Adm. fee) was built in 1857 with 17-foot ceilings, ornate plasterwork, and opulent furnishings; 1856 **Dunleith** (84 Homochitto St. 601-446-8500. Adm. fee) features restored outbuildings on its 40-acre grounds, while the house itself is surrounded by 26 tall, white columns; **Auburn** (400 Duncan Ave. 601-442-5981. Adm. fee) is known for its four front columns and a beautiful free-standing spiral staircase; and 1858 **Magnolia Hall** (215 S. Pearl St. 601-442-6672. Adm. fee) was the last mansion completed in Natchez before the Civil War.

Natchez Pilgrimage

Three times a year, some of Natchez's finest antebellum houses (including many not regularly open to the public) take part in "pilgrimage" tours, a tradition that dates back to the 1930s. Guides in period costumes welcome visitors to specially decorated homes, while the city hosts a variety of evening entertainment events. Exact dates vary from year to year, but the pilgrimages usually begin in early March, early October, and mid-December. For information call **Natchez Pilgrimage Tours** (601-446-6631 or 800-647-6742).

Hills and Delta

● **505 miles** ● **4 to 5 days** ● **Spring through fall**

Biking in Tishomingo State Park

It's too much, probably, to say that ghosts haunt the northern Mississippi landscape of this drive—but spirits surely do. The spirit of William Faulkner, who in his novels turned a fictional Yoknapatawpha County into a microcosm of the human condition, endures at his home in the university town of Oxford. At places along the peaceful Natchez Trace Parkway you can almost sense the presence of the pioneers who followed this path through the forested wilderness. The broad cotton fields of the delta evoke great blues singers like Robert Johnson of Greenwood. And, of course, Tupelo was the birthplace of a poor boy named Elvis, who blended blues, gospel, and hillbilly music into something that would reshape popular culture.

The route for this drive begins at a unique state park in the state's northeast corner and heads westward through Tupelo and Oxford to the bank of the Mississippi River before looping back again. You'll almost surely run

The King's birthplace, Elvis Presley Center in Tupelo

across a few surprises along the way, so pop in a tape of Elvis's greatest hits and get started.

Set in rolling uplands near the Alabama state line, **❶ Tishomingo State Park** *(Off Miss. 25, 2 miles S of Tishomingo. 601-438-6914. Adm. fee)* comes as a surprise to those who think of Mississippi as simply flat cotton fields and lazy bayous. Located in an outlying range of the Appalachian Mountains called the Tennessee River Hills, the park offers rocky hillsides, steep sandstone bluffs, hiking trails, and even a canoe trip *(mid-April–mid-Oct.; fee)* down Bear Creek. Tishomingo takes its name from a famous chief of the Chickasaw, the Native Americans who lived in the area until forced to move in the 1830s.

Leaving the park, head southwest on the **Natchez Trace Parkway**★ *(Headquarters 601-680-4025)*, a federally administered scenic road that meanders more than 400 miles from Natchez, Mississippi, to Nashville, Tennessee. The original Trace was probably just a pathway used by Indian hunters, but as time passed explorers and settlers began to use it to travel between the Mississippi and Tennessee Rivers. (Trace is a French word for track or trail.) In the flatboat era, boatmen walked or rode back northward along the Trace after a journey down the Ohio and Mississippi Rivers to Natchez or New Orleans, since their vessels usually were broken up and sold for lumber at the end of the trip. Today's parkway generally follows the historic route; in places you can actually walk part of the original Trace, worn deep into the earth by countless moccasins, boots, and horseshoes.

In the 50 miles between Tishomingo State Park and Tupelo you'll pass **Pharr Mounds,** a complex of eight Native American burial mounds dating from the time of Christ; **Donivan Slough,** a short nature trail through a wetland area; and **Dogwood Valley,** a trail winding among dogwood trees that bloom in early spring. At the parkway's **Tupelo Visitor Center** *(Milepost 266),* you'll find exhibits on Natchez Trace history, a bookstore, another nature trail, and rangers to answer your questions.

To thousands of people around the world, **Tupelo** *(Visitors Bureau, 399 E. Main St. 601-841-6521 or 800-533-0611)* is much more than just a small city in Mississippi: It's a place of pilgrimage, attracting busloads of visitors from

Maine to California, from Japan, Germany, Australia, and
all points in between.

On January 8, 1935, twin boys were born here to
Vernon and Gladys Presley. Jesse Garon died at birth, but
Elvis Aaron survived, learned to sing and play guitar,
recorded songs called "Heartbreak Hotel" and "Hound
Dog," and the world of music was never the same. At the
Elvis Presley Center *(306 Elvis Presley Dr. 601-841-1245.
Adm. fee),* you can walk through the tiny house where he
was born, visit a small museum displaying some of the
King's clothing, recordings, and other memorabilia, and
see the chapel built with donations from fans after his
death. True Elvis enthusiasts will want to take a driving
tour past his elementary school, his church, and the hard-
ware store where he bought his first guitar; maps are
available at the Visitors Bureau.

At the other end of town, the **Tupelo Museum**
*(W. Main St. in Ballard Park. 601-841-6438. Closed Mon.; adm.
fee)* is full of antiques, Indian artifacts, and Civil War items,
much of it housed in restored dairy barns. A reproduced
turn-of-the-century town includes an old country store,
radio station, and barbershop; among other exhibits are a
re-created Chickasaw
stick-and-mud hut and an
1873 dogtrot-style cabin.
The museum's space
hangar displays gear used
on NASA moon missions,
including a hatch cover
from Apollo 14 showing
meteorite marks.

Miss. 6 leads west
through the hills to
❷ Oxford *(Tourism
Council 601-234-4651 or
800-758-9177),* a town
that attracts a different
kind of pilgrim from the
Elvis-ophiles who flock
to Tupelo. This was the

William Faulkner's daughter, Jill Faulkner Summers, visiting Rowan Oak

home of Nobel Prize-winning novelist William Faulkner,
who wrote of a fictionalized Lafayette County in such
works as *Sartoris, The Sound and the Fury,* and *Absalom,
Absalom!* The house that was Faulkner's home and
refuge for the last 32 years of his life, **Rowan Oak** *(0.5
mile S of town square, on Old Taylor Rd. 601-234-3284. Closed
Mon.)* has been preserved just as it was when he died in
1962, with his Kodak on the mantel, and the outline for

Cotton fields along Miss. 6

A Fable written on the wall in his upstairs office. The home was built by an Irish immigrant in the 1840s; the cedars and magnolias in the yard date from about the same time. Also on the 32-acre grounds are a small horse barn (Faulkner kept horses and a series of stray dogs), an English "knot" garden, and a huge old muscadine vine, as tangled as the narrative in some of its former owner's novels.

Oxford is home to the **University of Mississippi** *(601-232-7378)*, founded in 1848 and better known (especially to football fans) as Ole Miss. The **University Museums** *(University Ave. 601-232-7073. Closed Mon.)* repay a visit with an outstanding collection of Greek and Roman artifacts, a fascinating display of 19th-century scientific instruments, and an important collection of southern folk art. If all this culture sparks a desire to learn more (about art, Faulkner, Oxford, or nearly anything else), drop by downtown's famed **Square Books** *(160 Courthouse Sq. 601-236-2262)*, where you can browse the shelves, admire the signed photos of writers, or sip a coffee on the upstairs porch overlooking the white-columned 1872 **Lafayette County Courthouse.**

West of Oxford on Miss. 6 it's time to take out the Elvis tape and put in some Muddy Waters or John Lee Hooker. You're leaving the hills and entering the flat farmland of the Delta, where early in this century the "field hollers" of cotton pickers merged with gospel to create a distinctly new African-American music called the blues. Clarksdale's **Delta Blues Museum** *(114 Delta Ave. 601-627-6820. Closed Sun.)*, upstairs at the public

Deer Creek, birthplace of Kermit the Frog

library, will help you understand the origins and development of blues music, from work songs to electrified Chicago-style blues. One of B.B. King's Gibson "Lucille" guitars is here, along with a well-worn 12-string that belonged to Big Joe Williams. Ask here for venues around town where you can hear live blues on weekends.

Miss. 1 is part of the **Great River Road,** a system of highways running the length of the Mississippi—but as you drive through the cotton fields here you may wonder just where the Big Muddy is. In fact, it's on the other side of the levee to the west; to get a look at it, stop in at ❸ **Great River Road State Park** *(Miss. 1 and Miss. 8. 601-759-6762. Adm. fee)* near Rosedale. Beyond a nature trail and the Visitor Center is an observation tower where you can look out over broad sandbars to the river. At various times of the year you may see bald eagles, herons, egrets, terns, or pelicans, and there's nearly always a barge chugging by.

Farther south, **Winterville Mounds Museum State Park** *(Miss. 1. 601-334-4684. Wed.-Sun.; adm. fee)* protects the site of a major group of Native American ceremonial mounds. The flat-topped structures are thought to have been built about A.D. 1000 by the predecessors of the Choctaw and Chickasaw, and were probably topped with temples or chiefs' houses; archaeologists believe the site was occupied for about six centuries. The museum contains artifacts and interpretive exhibits on the mound builders.

Beyond Greenville, take Miss. 12 east to **Leroy Percy State Park** *(601-827-5436. Adm. fee),* a reminder of what this region looked like before European settlement. The Mississippi River Alluvial Plain was once among the most diverse and productive ecosystems on the continent: Its bottomland-hardwood forests were renewed by flooding each year, its mucky soil the basis of a food chain that ended in such predators as black bear, panthers, alligators, and eagles. But the huge old trees were too tempting not to be cut, the soil too rich not to be cleared and plowed.

Today, the vast bottomland forests are nearly all gone, the populations of native plants and animals a fraction of what they once were. At places like Leroy Percy, though, you can experience a bit of the past, walking under tall oaks and bald cypresses draped in Spanish moss, listening to the calls of flycatchers, vireos, and warblers, or to the high scream of a red-shouldered hawk.

One of Mississippi's most unusual and delightful museums is located in a small house in **Belzoni,** a town best known for its catfish industry (see sidebar this page). To ward off depression after her husband died, Ethel Wright Mohamed began, at age 60, to embroider scenes from her

109

life, recalling the couple's happy times. Her work is now displayed at **Mama's Dream World** *(307 Central St. 601-247-1433. Call for appt.; adm. fee),* where the walls are covered with dozens of stitchery images of American history, old sayings, mythology, and dreams, jumbled together in eccentric and symbolic combinations. During her lifetime Mohamed was one of Mississippi's most honored folk artists, and her work is represented in the Smithsonian Institution's Textile Division.

For a trip back to the antebellum era, take Miss. 7 and US 82 to ❹ **Greenwood** *(Visitors Bureau 601-453-9197 or 800-748-9064)* and visit **Florewood River Plantation** *(2 miles W of town, off US 82. 601-455-3821. March-Nov. Tues.-Sun., limited tours Dec.-Feb.; adm. fee),* a re-created 1850s cotton plantation on the bank of the Yazoo River. A planter's mansion and more than 20 outbuildings—including cookhouse, sewing house, and slave quarters—depict a self-sufficient community where 80 slaves would have worked fields of cotton and corn. The planter's house is more modest (and therefore more typical of the times) than many of the grand mansions seen in period movies; its furnishings include a half-tester bed and a "wig dresser" that belonged to famed Confederate Gen. Nathan Bedford Forrest.

Despite its name, Greenwood's **Cottonlandia Museum** *(US 82. 601-453-0925. Adm. fee)* covers much more than agriculture. Among the many exhibits here are an extensive collection of Indian pottery and tools, a display of 16th-century Spanish glass trade beads, and a mastodon skeleton found locally. Civil War relics include items retrieved from the gunboat *Star of the West,* scuttled in the Tallahatchie River in 1863.

Costumed interpreter, Florewood River Plantation

At Starkville, turn south to **Noxubee National Wildlife Refuge** *(Off Oktoc Rd. 601-323-5548),* one of the state's finest areas for wildlife observation. The diverse habitats on the refuge's 47,000 acres include lakes, bottomland forest, and pines, providing homes for a long list of species. Winter brings thousands of waterfowl, while in spring the woods can ring with the calls of songbirds. Alligators are active on the lakes in the warm months, and you may come across a white-tailed deer or wild turkey anytime.

Playwright Tennessee Williams was born in 1911 in historic **5 Columbus,** east on US 82; the 1878 Victorian house that was his birthplace is now the city's **Welcome Center** *(300 E. Main St. 601-328-0222),* where you can pick up walking and driving guides to the area. Columbus suffered little damage in the Civil War, and dozens of impressive antebellum houses still stand. (Most of the houses are privately owned, although some are open limited times for tours; check at the Welcome Center for details.) Among the most notable houses are the Italianate 1847 **Lee Home** *(316 7th St.),* once the residence of Confederate Gen. Stephen D. Lee; the 1848 **Amzi Love House** *(305 7th St. S.);* and the ornate 1857 **White Arches** *(122 7th St. S.),* a blend of Gothic, Greek Revival, and Italianate styles.

Just north of Columbus, turn off US 45 onto Miss. 50 west to reach magnificent **Waverly Plantation Mansion** *(601-494-1399. Adm. fee),* built in 1852 near the Tombigbee River. The imposing 8,000-square-foot Greek Revival house is best known for its 65-foot-high central rotunda, surrounded by curved

Waverly Plantation Mansion near Columbus

111

stairways and balconies lined with 718 mahogany spindles. Waverly sat empty from 1913 to 1962, but incredibly still possesses original chandeliers and plaster ceiling medallions and much of its original glass. After a long restoration, it's now mended and polished and filled with fine antiques—ready, it seems, to host a fancy ball.

Like Columbus, **Aberdeen** encompasses many fine antebellum houses, some of which are open for tours by prior arrangement. Aberdeen's Franklin Street was called "Silk Stocking Avenue" for its many impressive residences, such as **Shadowlawn** *(303 S. Franklin St.),* an Italianate home built in 1863. **Holliday Haven** *(609 S. Meridian St.),* an 1850 Greek Revival house, also ranks among the city's most notable structures. For information and a driving guide, stop at the Visitors Bureau in **The Magnolias** *(732 W. Commerce St. 601-369-9440 or 800-634-3538. Mon.-Fri.),* an 1850 Greek Revival mansion fronted by a mini-allée of magnolias and graced inside by a three-level mahogany double stairway and a ghost named Miss Maggie.

Little Rock and the Delta

● **420 miles** ● **3 to 4 days** ●**Year-round**

See p. 128

See p. 105

Geographically speaking, Arkansas is a state divided: In the west and northwest rise rugged mountains and rolling hills; to the east the land stretches for miles as flat as an ironing board. Little Rock, Arkansas's capital and largest city, lies at the precise juncture of upland and lowland, making it a convenient starting point for exploring either region.

Just Don't Say "Arkie"

What do you call somebody from Arkansas? Most people say "Arkansan," with the accent on the second syllable. But a significant minority of residents object on the ground that the state's name isn't ar-KAN-sas, and besides, it sounds too much like "Kansan." Some of the state's leading historians and writers prefer "Arkansawyer," and stubbornly hold out for that honorably antique term in speech and print.

This drive heads eastward, winding through the alluvial plain of the Mississippi River, commonly called the "Delta" by Southerners—never mind that the mighty river's true delta is in Louisiana, hundreds of miles to the southeast. The route traverses flat agricultural land as it visits Stuttgart, famed for duck hunting and rice, and the cotton city of Pine Bluff. After pausing in Helena, on the bank of the Mississippi, it follows the geological curiosity known as Crowleys Ridge, a strip of high ground roughly paralleling the river. Little of the drive could be called scenic (unless you particularly admire rice and soybean fields), but its stops are rich in history, from Native American sites far predating European exploration to Civil War battlefields. Then, too, beauty isn't entirely lacking: Several natural areas afford excellent wildlife viewing, their swamps and woods offering a taste of what the landscape was like before the arrival of the sawmill, the plow, and the automobile.

As European explorers traveled up the Arkansas River, the first true high ground they encountered was marked by a stone outcropping on the south bank. This "little rock" eventually became the site of the region's major settlement, located at the crossroads of two principal

pioneer routes: the Southwest Trail from
St. Louis, Missouri, to Texas, and the river itself. Early
times in **❶ Little Rock** *(Visitors Bureau 501-376-4781 or
800-844-4781)* are re-created at the **Arkansas Territorial
Restoration** *(200 E. 3rd St. 501-324-9351. Adm. fee)*, which
includes the 1820s Hinderliter Grog Shop, the city's oldest
still-standing structure; guides in period costume give
tours of this and several other 19th-century buildings. At
the nearby **Museum of Discovery** *(500 E. Markham St. 501-
396-7050. Scheduled to open in 1998; adm. fee)*, exhibits range
from the region's Paleo-Indian inhabitants to contemporary scientific topics.

Walk a few blocks west to the **Old State House**★
(300 W. Markham St. 501-324-9685), one of Arkansas's most
venerable and strikingly handsome buildings. Fronted by
four grand Doric columns, this Greek Revival masterpiece
served as Arkansas's State Capitol from 1836 to 1911, and
now houses varied historical exhibits. Its significance
does not lie entirely in the distant past, though: Bill Clinton made his presidential victory speeches on its lawn in
both 1992 and 1996. While you're in the neighborhood,
take a look at the beautifully restored lobby of the 1877
Capital Hotel *(111 W. Markham St. 501-374-7474)*, as
glittering now as when it
hosted such notables as
Ulysses S. Grant.

You'll find one of the
city's most rewarding attractions in **MacArthur Park** *(9th
St., near I-30)*, named for Gen.
Douglas MacArthur, who
was born in an 1841 military
arsenal here. The **Arkansas
Arts Center** *(9th and Commercial Sts. 501-372-4000. Donation)* is renowned for its
collection of drawings and
prints. The Arts Center's **Decorative Arts Museum** *(7th
and Rock Sts. 501-372-4000)* is

Historic Quapaw Quarter, Little Rock

well worth a visit not only for its exhibits of ornamental
objects but for its location in the 1840 Greek Revival Pike-
Fletcher-Terry House, once owned by the eccentric 19th-
century soldier-poet Albert Pike.

Little Rock's **Quapaw Quarter** neighborhood, south of
downtown, is dotted with impressively restored Victorian
houses. Check with the **Quapaw Quarter Association**
(1315 S. Scott St. 501-371-0075. Mon.-Fri.) for driving guides.

Riverboat docked at Little Rock's Riverfront Park

Most houses are private, but **Villa Marie** *(1321 S. Scott St. 501-374-9979. Closed Sat.; adm. fee)* offers tours of its authentically furnished interior. The 1881 Italianate house gained notoriety when its exterior served as the setting for the popular television series *Designing Women.*

If you'd like one last look at hills before heading into the Delta, take Ark. 10 west to Ark. 300 and visit **Pinnacle Mountain State Park** *(501-868-5806);* Pinnacle's pinnacle provides a fine panorama of the Arkansas River, the foothills of the Ouachitas, and Lake Maumelle. The .75-mile trail to the summit is moderately strenuous; nearby Kingfisher Trail—flat, paved, and easy—wanders a half mile along Little Maumelle River past towering bald cypresses.

Take US 165 southeast to the hamlet of Scott, where the **Plantation Agriculture Museum** *(US 165 and Ark. 161. 501-961-1409. Closed Mon.; adm. fee)* re-creates the era when cotton was king in the South, depicting its cultivation from plowing to ginning to baling. Exhibits on plantation life include a re-created mule barn interior. Proceed 4 miles on US 165 to **Toltec Mounds Archeological State Park** *(490 Toltec Mounds Rd. 501-961-9442. Closed Mon.; adm. fee),* which preserves a prehistoric Native American ceremonial center. The name Toltec (a Mexican civilization) was mistakenly given to the mounds by a 19th-century owner; in truth, the mounds were constructed from about A.D. 700 to 1025 by a people known as the Plum Bayou Culture. As you study the village's scale model in the Visitor Center, note that these mounds, like many others in the region, seem to have been aligned according to astronomical observations; a walking tour route leads past the major mounds to an oxbow lake of the Arkansas River.

Continue eastward on US 165 to **Stuttgart** *(Chamber of Commerce 870-673-1602),* a small town that calls itself, with justification, the "rice and duck capital of the world." Surrounding rice fields and swampy woods host impressive flocks of wintering waterfowl, and each November the

Wings Over the Prairie Festival includes the World's Championship Duck Calling Contest, a hard-fought competition that attracts expert quackers from all over North America.

Visit the excellent **Stuttgart Agricultural Museum** *(921 E. 4th St. 870-673-7001. Closed Mon.; donation)* to view a collection of agricultural tools and household items depicting pioneer life on Arkansas's Grand Prairie (see sidebar p. 117). A re-created downtown street, with post office, doctor's office, and general mercantile, adds to the museum's appeal; among the farming implements are ditchers and levelers used in early rice farming and an enormous steam traction engine, ancestor of today's high-tech tractors. In the wildlife exhibit area you can even take a computerized duck hunt and learn the calls of several species of waterfowl.

Take US 79 southwest to ❷ **Pine Bluff** *(Convention & Visitors Bureau 870-536-7600 or 800-536-7660),* where your first stop should be the **Dexter Harding House** *(110 N. Pine St. 870-536-7606. Mon.-Fri.),* an 1850 structure moved to this location and now serving as the Tourist Informa-

tion Center. Here you'll learn of several notable sites in this railroad and cotton-farming city, including the **Arts and Science Center for Southeast Arkansas** *(701 Main St. 870-536-3375),* which hosts changing exhibitions; the **Arkansas Railroad Museum** *(Port Rd., off US 65. 870-535-8819. Closed Sun.),* where the star attraction is the splendidly restored and

Pine Bluff mural

hugely impressive steam locomotive No. 819; and the **Pine Bluff-Jefferson County Historical Museum** *(201 E. 4th Ave. 870-541-5402. Closed Sun.),* located in the city's renovated Union Station. Don't miss the unique **Band Museum** *(423 Main St. 870-534-4676. Closed Sun.),* which not only features historic musical instruments but tempts you into its back room for a treat at a restored 1950s-style soda fountain. Ask at the Tourist Information Center for a guide to Pine Bluff's many **downtown murals,** illustrating scenes from local history on a giant-size scale.

Follow US 65 south to Gould and turn east on

Ark. 212 and north on US 165, where you'll find the birthplace of Arkansas. **Arkansas Post National Memorial** *(Ark. 169. 870-548-2207)* commemorates the region's first European settlement, founded by French explorer Henri de Tonti in 1686 on the bank of the Arkansas River. A Visitor Center and self-guided walking tour cover the town's influential history, from trading post to military fort to territorial capital to Civil War battleground—to, finally, decline and abandonment after Little Rock took over as the state's major city. Stop at the nearby **Arkansas Post Museum** *(US 165 and Ark. 169. 870-548-2634. Adm. fee)* for an interesting collection of restored buildings, including a 19th-century dogtrot house, and varied local historical items. One prize is an original 1819 edition of the *Arkansas Gazette*, Arkansas's first newspaper, founded at Arkansas Post.

Arkansas Post National Memorial, on the bank of the Arkansas River

Continue north on US 165 to Ark. 1, where the ❸ **White River National Wildlife Refuge** *(Refuge office, 321 W. 7th St., DeWitt. 870-946-1468)* ranks as one of the state's finest natural areas: 157,000 acres of hardwood forest and wetlands teeming with wildlife from black bears and bald eagles to dozens of species of songbirds. Only a small part of the refuge is accessible by car; before you begin exploring check at the office for maps and advice. Some roads are closed seasonally, and even when they're open they can be muddy and difficult.

Take Ark. 1 north to US 49, where a short side trip north meanders to **Louisiana Purchase State Park** *(Ark. 362)*, a small preserve of both natural and historical interest. Here a boardwalk winds through a swamp of bald cypress and water tupelo. At its end a monument marks the zero point from which the original surveyors of the Louisiana Purchase began plotting the vast new addition to our nation in 1815, 12 years after Thomas Jefferson bought it from France.

Recalling his steamboat days on the Mississippi, Mark Twain once wrote that ❹ **Helena** *(Tourism Commission 870-338-9831)* occupied "one of the prettiest situations on the Mississippi"—a high-class testimonial indeed. These days, the thousands who attend the **King Biscuit Blues Festival** in October are less concerned with scenery than with the great music performed on several stages along Cherry Street. The festival, annually presenting an extensive lineup of new and established blues artists, is Helena's major attraction, but the town deserves a visit the rest of the year, too. Don't miss the **Delta Cultural Center** *(95 Missouri St. 870-338-4350)*, located in a renovated 1912 train depot; exhibits illustrating life in eastern Arkansas include a reprise of *King Biscuit Time*, the historic radio show that began broadcasting from Helena in 1941 (and later provided a name for the blues festival). An important Civil War battle was fought in Helena on July 4, 1863, the same day Vicksburg fell to Union forces; some of the victims are buried in the hilltop **Confederate Cemetery** *(1801 Holly St.)*, where you'll find a fine view of the Mississippi below. Local historical items, including Civil War memorabilia and Native American artifacts, are the focus of the **Phillips County Museum** *(623 Pecan St. 870-338-7790. Tues.-Sat.)*.

The route gets a little more complicated now, following Ark. 242, Forest Service Road 1900 *(gravel; inquire locally before driving)*, and Ark. 44, but the reward is the attractive woodland of **St. Francis National Forest** *(870-295-5278)*, located on Crowleys Ridge, a long, narrow strip of high ground that runs from Helena north into Missouri. Camping and swimming *(fees for both)* are popular at Forest Service campgrounds at **Bear Creek Lake** and **Storm Creek Lake.**

Take Ark. 284 north from Forrest City to the finest natural treasure of the ridge, **Village Creek State Park**★ *(201 Cty. Rd. 754. 870-238-9406)*, where you can fish, swim, or camp in the beautifully natural surroundings of Arkansas's largest state park. You can also hike a section of the historic Old Military Road that ran from Memphis to Little Rock. This and other park trails pass through lush forest with a mix of species unique to Crowleys Ridge,

Grand Prairie

When European settlers came to Arkansas, they found an expanse of tall-grass prairie covering a half million acres stretching northward from Arkansas Post. The "Grand Prairie," as pioneers called it, was located mostly in what are now Arkansas and Prairie Counties. Shortly after the turn of the century, farmers discovered that the prairie's water-retaining clay soil was perfect for rice cultivation; as a result, essentially the entire ecosystem has now been displaced by agriculture and other development. (As a further result, Arkansas is the leading rice-producing state in America.) To see remnants of virgin prairie, drive along US 70 between Carlisle and De Valls Bluff, or ask at the Stuttgart Agricultural Museum for directions to 40-acre Roth Prairie, just south of town.

117

including tulip tree, butternut, beech, cucumber magnolia, and sugar maple.

Drive east on US 64 to Ark. 184 and ❺ **Parkin Archeological State Park** *(Visitor Center, 60 Ark. 184. 870-755-2500. Closed Mon.; adm. fee),* a site on the St. Francis River whose importance belies its modest size. Where the park's small but well-designed museum now stands, a thriving Native American village of the Mississippian Culture existed from about A.D. 1000 to 1550. Based on physical and written evidence, archaeologists believe this site was the town of Casqui (named for an important chief), which was visited by Spanish explorer Hernando de Soto in 1541. In summer you may see an excavation in progress here, and at any time of year you'll enjoy the wonderfully evocative pottery and other artifacts displayed in the museum.

Fishing the White River, near St. Charles

Continue east on US 64 to Marion, and go north on I-55 to Ark. 42 and the **Wapanocca National Wildlife Refuge** *(Off Ark. 42, near Turrell. 870-343-2595).* Birdwatchers drive its 6-mile auto route to see geese, ducks, and hawks in winter, and wetland-loving birds in summer.

Before returning to Little Rock, amble north on US 63 to ❻ **Jonesboro** *(Chamber of Commerce 870-932-6691),* home of the admirable **Arkansas State University Museum** *(Off Caraway Rd. 870-972-2074);* here you'll find significant Native American artifacts, military items, and a major collection of glassware. The museum's Old Town Arkansas exhibit re-creates a turn-of-the-century village, including a post office, general store, print shop, and doctor's office (with a very scary looking early X-ray machine).

Hot Springs and the Ouachitas ★

● **630 miles** ● **4 to 6 days** ● **Year-round** ● **Watch for log trucks in timberland.**

Compared with the Ozarks to the north, the Ouachitas are Arkansas's "other" mountains, too often over-looked by vacationers and outdoorspeople. Yet within or near these largely unpeopled hills can be found a fine diversity of attractions: some of the most rugged terrain in the central United States, the South's largest national forest, Arkansas's largest lake and highest mountain, a famed scenic byway, a historic spa city, the birthplace of a presi-

See p. 128

dent, and—of all improbable things—a park where you can pick up real diamonds right off the ground.

The drive begins in Hot Springs National Park, long a favorite recreation spot, and heads southwest through Hope, President Bill Clinton's hometown. After stopping at Texarkana, straddling the Arkansas-Texas state line, you'll then turn back north through the Ouachita Mountains to the historic city of Fort Smith, situated on the Oklahoma border. From here you'll follow the Arkansas River Valley eastward, cresting the state's highest peak and visiting several excellent natural areas before returning to the start.

According to legend, Native Americans agreed that the thermal waters at ❶ **Hot Springs** (*Visitors Bureau 501-321-2277 or 800-772-2489*) would be neutral territory, so bathers from any tribe could relax and enjoy a good soak without having to be on the alert for enemies. That tradition continued, in a manner of speaking, into the 20th century, when gangsters like Al Capone, celebrities like

Fordyce Bathhouse along Bathhouse Row, Hot Springs

Babe Ruth, and politicians like Harry Truman came to town to mingle with tourists and local folks, and nobody worried about anything but good times and a hot bath. (The city's spirit of laissez-faire also led to the establishment of several gambling clubs, which operated here openly, though illegally, until the late 1960s.)

The supposed healing powers of the hot springs' 143°F water made them a mecca for the variously afflicted in the early 1800s, and in 1832 Congress declared the land around the springs a federal reservation—the first in American history. In 1921 this reserve became **Hot Springs National Park** (*369 Central Ave. 501-624-3383*), today one of the country's most unusual: 5,549 acres of parkland entwined with commercial and residential areas of the city of Hot Springs, blending history, geology, and natural beauty with restaurants, souvenir shops, and art galleries.

The eight impressive buildings of **Bathhouse Row** (*Central Ave.*) are reminders of the glory years of "taking the waters"; the fact that most stand empty and unused testifies to the decline of therapeutic bathing. Stop at the **Fordyce Bathhouse**★ (*369 Central Ave.*), a beautifully restored 1915 Renaissance Revival structure now serving as the national park Visitor Center, for an overview of the springs and park. Guided or self-guided tours lead through elegant parlors, bath halls, a gymnasium, and a steam room that claimed to treat "rheumatism, advanced syphilis, jaundice, and obesity." While the 1912 **Buckstaff** (*509 Central Ave. 501-623-2308. Closed Sun.; fee for bathing*) is the only traditional bathhouse still operating, several hotels offer the service with water piped in from the springs.

Although he was born in Hope, 80 miles away, future President Bill Clinton moved to Hot Springs when he was seven and grew up here; a driving tour brochure available at the city's **Visitor Information Center** (*629 Central Ave. 501-321-9763 or 800-543-2284*) leads you past his two homes, his church, his high school, and even the site of his bowling alley.

Just a short distance from Bathhouse Row is the headquarters of the **Ouachita National Forest** (*100 Reserve St. 501-321-5202. Office closed weekends*), where you can pick up maps and guides to camping and recreation areas. Covering 1.7 million acres, Ouachita is the largest national forest in the South, comprising 26 campgrounds in Arkansas (with others in Oklahoma), 7 wilderness areas, and extensive hiking trails.

West of downtown via US 270, **Mid-America Science Museum** *(500 Mid-America Blvd., off Ark. 227. 501-767-3461. Mem. Day–Labor Day daily, Tues.-Sun. rest of year; adm. fee)* is a kinetic, colorful, hands-on place that uses interactive exhibits to explain everything from electricity to erosion. Kids and adults alike will enjoy the "Featherstone-Kite Openwork Basketweave Mark II Gentleman's Flying Machine," an amazingly wacky contraption built by Sir Roland Emmett, creator of the props for the movie *Chitty Chitty Bang Bang*. Continuing north on Ark. 227, you'll reach **Lake Ouachita State Park** *(5451 Mountain Pine Rd. 501-767-9366)*, on the shore of 48,000-acre **Lake Ouachita**, Arkansas's largest lake and a favorite of anglers, water-skiers, and scuba divers. The state park includes a marina with boat rentals, a swimming area, hiking trails, and cabins; the lake is ringed with U.S. Army Corps of Engineers recreation areas.

121

Return to US 270 west to Mount Ida, then follow Ark. 27 south. At Salem, detour west on Ark. 84 and Ark. 369 to two of the forest's prettiest areas: At **Albert Pike Recreation Area** you can camp or fish amid a pine-hardwood forest on the Little Missouri River, a

Mule-drawn trolley in Hot Springs

lovely, clear stream perfect for swimming on a hot summer day; at nearby **Little Missouri Falls** the river cascades over rugged rock ledges.

Ark. 27 leads southward from Salem to Murfreesboro and ❷ **Crater of Diamonds State Park** ★ *(2 miles S of Murfreesboro, on Ark. 301. 870-285-3113)*, a spot that truly deserves the much abused adjective "unique." At the center of the park is a 36.5-acre expanse of igneous rock containing diamonds—genuine, honest-to-goodness gems—brought to the surface by ancient volcanic activity

Hunting for diamonds at Crater of Diamonds State Park

Genuine Arkansas diamond

Downscale Diamonds

Though the gems at **Crater of Diamonds State Park** are real, the "Arkansas diamonds" you see promoted at roadside souvenir stands are actually quartz crystals, found in abundance in the Ouachita Mountains. Around 270 million years ago, conditions were right for the formation of crystals in these hills: Source rock provided silica, the basic mineral; flowing water dissolved the material; and fractures in the rock provided spaces for the crystals to grow. Today, quartz crystals are sought both commercially and by weekend rockhounds. In the 1980s, at the height of the New Age movement, crystals were often purported to possess magical "healing" or "channeling" powers, and the Ouachitas were a magnet for true believers.

and accessible to all who pay a small search fee. An average of one or two diamonds are found every day at the park, the only publicly accessible diamond field in North America. Most are small, but dreams of past finds like the 40-carat Uncle Sam and the 34-carat Star of Murfreesboro keep visitors searching for a big payoff.

Farther south on Ark. 27 at Nashville, take Ark. 4 southeast to **Old Washington Historic State Park**★ *(870-983-2684 or 870-983-2733. Fee for tours),* a collection of historically significant buildings that were saved by a town's decline in fortune. A thriving stop on the old Southwest Trail, Washington became the Confederate capital of Arkansas after Little Rock was occupied by Union forces in 1863. But the Cairo and Fulton Railroad passed a few miles east in 1874, beginning Washington's fall, and two devastating fires in the next decade accelerated the trend.

Today visitors can tour many of the park's more than 30 historic buildings, including the 1845 Greek Revival Royston House; the 1832 federal-style Block House; and the 1836 Hempstead County Courthouse, which served as the state's Confederate capitol. Several structures have been moved to the park from elsewhere, such as the 1832 Williams Tavern, now the park restaurant. One of Washington's most famous residents was blacksmith James Black, whom legend credits with having created the original Bowie knife. The fearsomely long-bladed weapon was made famous by soldier-adventurer Jim Bowie, who died at the Alamo in 1836. The park's blacksmith shop, a modern re-creation, recalls Black and those rowdy pioneer days.

On August 19, 1946, a boy named William Jefferson Blythe IV was born in **Hope** *(Chamber of Commerce 870-777-3640)* to a woman whose husband had been killed three months earlier in an automobile accident. When his mother remarried, young Bill became a Clinton, the name he used when he was sworn in as the 42nd President in 1993. The **Clinton Birthplace** *(117 S. Hervey St. 870-777-4455. March-Sept. Tues.-Sun., Oct.-Feb. Tues.-Sat.; adm. fee)*, the two-story wood frame house where he lived until the age of four, displays memorabilia and furnishings from the 1930s through 1950s. Stop in at the **Hope Visitor Center and Museum** *(S. Main and Division Sts. 870-722-2580)* in the restored train depot downtown. The museum has displays on Clinton and other local history, as well as a driving guide to local presidential-related sites.

Clinton Birthplace, Hope

Until Bill Clinton became President, Hope was best known for its annual **Watermelon Festival** *(Contact Chamber of Commerce)*, celebrating the fact that some of the world's biggest melons are grown in the area. The festival, which takes place the third weekend in August, is a good time to visit, when the sweet fruits are ripe and ready for the knife.

Refusing to play favorites, **9** **Texarkana** *(Chamber of*

Little Missouri Falls in autumn

Commerce 903-792-7191) calls itself "Texarkana, U.S.A.,"
rather than Texas or Arkansas. In front of the post office
on State Line Avenue is a special spot where thousands of
travelers have had their pictures taken with one foot in
Texas and the other in Arkansas. The nearby **Ace of
Clubs House** (420 Pine St. 903-793-4831. Tues.-Sat.; adm.
fee), an 1885 Italianate residence, is elegantly furnished
with items from the late 19th and early 20th centuries.
The house's unusual name and shape are explained by
an even more unusual story: The first owner is said to
have won a small fortune by drawing the ace of clubs in
a high-stakes poker game. With the pot he built a home
in the shape of the club design on a playing card.

The home of the **Texarkana Historical Museum** (219
N. State Line Ave. 903-793-4831. Tues.-Sat.; adm. fee) has a
more ordinary origin but an equally impressive form, with
a tall turret gracing one corner of a brick 1879 former
bank building. Inside, exhibits include Caddo Indian artifacts, a Victorian parlor, and displays on the great ragtime
composer Scott Joplin, who was born in Texarkana in
1868. The beautifully restored **Perot Theatre** (221 Main St.
903-792-4992) doesn't have a regular tour schedule, but
call for information about getting a look inside this neo-
Renaissance showplace—or, better yet, attend one of the
concerts, ballets, dramas, or musicals offered here.

Take US 71 north to Ashdown, where birders and
anglers will want to make a side trip east on Ark. 32 to

29,500-acre **Millwood Lake** *(U.S. Army Corps of Engineers office 870-898-3343)*. Fishing is good any time of year, but birdwatchers flock to the lake mostly in fall and winter, when its stump-studded waters host thousands of ducks, grebes, gulls, loons, cormorants, and pelicans. Bald eagles regularly nest at Millwood, one of the few places in Arkansas where the big raptors breed. The U.S. Army Corps of Engineers provides camping on the lake, as does **Millwood State Park** *(1564 Ark. 32. 870-898-2800)*.

Continuing north on US 71 to Mena, take Ark. 88 west, which is the **Talimena Scenic Byway★**, one of the most spectacular drives between the Appalachians and the Rockies. Winding along Ouachita Mountains ridgetops for 54 miles between Mena and Talihina, Oklahoma, the drive reaches its highest point on 2,681-foot Rich Mountain, but there are splendid panoramic views of forested hills at overlooks all along the way. Here you'll see graphic evidence of how the Ouachitas were created some 300 million years ago, squeezed together by tectonic forces that caused massive "wrinkles" in the earth's surface, forming long east-west ridges with narrow intervening valleys. At several spots you'll note tilted rock strata, testifying to the powerful geological forces once at work here.

The lodge and restaurant at ❹ **Queen Wilhelmina State Park** *(Talimena Scenic Byway, 3877 Ark. 88. 501-394-2863 or 800-264-2477)* make a fine overnight or mealtime break. The modern lodge is the third to stand on the mountaintop here; the first, financed by Dutch railroad interests, was named for the then-queen of the Netherlands, and the name has carried on through the years.

Farther north of Mena on US 71, ❺ **Fort Smith★** has a long and illustrious past, beginning with the establishment of a military outpost in 1817 at the confluence of the Poteau and Arkansas Rivers. Today's **Fort Smith National Historic Site** *(Rogers Ave. and 3rd St. 501-783-3961. Courtroom and jail closed for restoration until fall 1999; adm. fee)* centers on an 1851 Army barracks that housed the courtroom of federal Judge Isaac C. Parker, an iron-willed man who from 1875 to 1896 worked to bring order to the adjacent Indian Territory (now Oklahoma)—and sent 79 criminals to the gallows while doing it. ("I never hanged a man," Parker once said. "It was the law.") The jail under Parker's courtroom was called "Hell on the Border"; you can see foundations of the original 1817 fort, the 1846 commissary, and

Scarecrows near Mansfield

a re-creation of the gallows where the condemned met their fates at the end of a rope.

The nearby **Old Fort Museum** *(320 Rogers Ave. 501-783-7841. Closed Mon.; adm. fee)* contains exhibits on Fort Smith history from its earliest days, when soldiers tried to keep the peace between the Osage and Cherokee, through the Civil War and into the modern era. Highlights include a wonderful old horse-drawn fire wagon and a 1920s drugstore with glass cases full of strange cure-alls.

The city's **Visitor Center** *(2 N. B St. 501-783-8888 or 800-637-1477)* has its own colorful history: The 1890s building was once officially the River Front Hotel, but locals simply called it "Miss Laura's Social Club," for the madam who ran it as a brothel. The exterior features striking oeils-de-boeuf, and the interior has been playfully restored in keeping with its shady-lady past.

The **Belle Grove Historic District** *(Bounded by North*

Fort Smith National Historic Site

5th, North H, North 8th, and North C Sts. Self-guided tour brochure available at Fort Smith Visitor Center) encompasses many historic structures. Among them is the **Clayton House** *(514 N. 6th St. 501-783-3000. Wed.-Sun.; adm. fee),* built in the 1850s and later owned and enlarged by W.H.H. Clayton, district attorney during Judge Parker's era. Today the house is a showplace of period furnishings, including some Clayton family possessions. A block away, the **Fort Smith Art Center** *(423 N. 6th St. 501-784-2787. Tues.-Sat.)* is located in an 1857 brick Second Empire-style house where soldiers were billeted during the Civil War.

The **Darby House** *(311 N. 8th St. 501-782-3388. Mon.-Fri.)* contains memorabilia of Gen. William O. Darby, who grew up here and later founded "Darby's Rangers," a famed fighting unit active in Italy during World War II.

Just across the Arkansas River in **Van Buren** *(Chamber of Commerce 501-474-2761)* you'll find a nicely restored Main Street of two- and three-story redbrick buildings. Stop first at the 1901 **Old Frisco Depot** *(813 Main St.)*, now the city's Chamber of Commerce, for a walking tour brochure, and then head down the street past the circa 1892 **Anheuser-Busch Brewing Company** *(600 Main St.)*, the turn-of-the-century **King Opera House** *(427 Main St.)*, and the 1877 **Crawford County Courthouse** *(300 block of Main St.)*, with its clock tower and 1830s log schoolhouse moved to the courthouse square from a site about a mile away.

Take Ark. 59 and Ark. 22 to Paris, and follow twisting Ark. 309—officially the **Mount Magazine Scenic Byway** of the **Ozark National Forest** *(501-968-2354)*—over the top of Magazine Mountain, the state's highest peak. A new state park is under development on Magazine Mountain, which offers grand lookouts around its rim road. The actual high point, called Signal Hill, is reached by the short Signal Hill Trail, which tops out at 2,753 feet above sea level.

Leaving the national forest, follow Ark. 10, 27, 154, and 155 to **Holla Bend National Wildlife Refuge** *(3 miles E of Centerville. 501-229-4300. Adm. fee)*, one of Arkansas's finest and most accessible natural areas. Located within an old channel of the Arkansas River, the 6,486-acre refuge is home to thousands of wintering ducks and geese, as well as bald eagles, hawks, and owls. A drive around the 8-mile tour road any time of year may turn up a coyote, armadillo, bobcat, white-tailed deer, or wild turkey.

Take care on Ark. 154 as it winds its tortuous way up from the Arkansas River bottomland to ❻ **Petit Jean State Park** *(13 miles E of Centerville on Ark. 154. 501-727-5441)*, atop Petit Jean Mountain. The ascent is dizzying, but the reward is worthwhile: Petit Jean's lodge and cabins *(501-727-5431)*, hiking trails, fishing lake, and excellent scenery make it one of Arkansas's most popular parks. Don't miss the hike from Mather Lodge to Cedar Falls, a fairly strenuous round-trip of 2.2 miles to a 95-foot waterfall dropping into a pool almost encircled by rock walls. Near the park, the **Museum of Automobiles** *(Jones Lane, off Ark. 154. 501-727-5427. Adm. fee)* offers a varied collection of beautifully restored antique cars, including a 1967 Ford Mustang convertible owned by Bill Clinton.

Return to Hot Springs via Ark. 9 and Ark. 5.

What We Meant Was...

Every state has a few funny place-names, and Arkansas certainly has its share, from Oil Trough to Toad Suck to Hogeye. A few miles east of Mena is the small town of **Ink,** which may well boast the most interesting origin for its moniker. When the town sought a post office (so the story goes), the government sent a form with a space for the applicants to fill in the town name. "Write in ink," the instructions said so they did.

**● 310 miles (with side trips) ● 4 to 5 days
● Spring through fall ● Fall foliage can be
spectacular. Occasional winter storms make
driving hazardous in the mountains.**

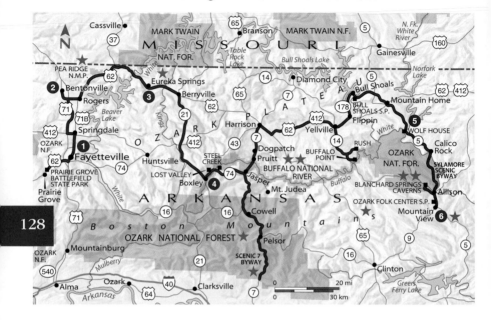

The Europeans who settled Arkansas found the rich
alluvial soil of the flat eastern section far more inviting
than the rugged mountains and deep "hollers" of the
northwest. In those early days, too, rivers were the most
important mode of transportation, and waterways in the
rocky uplands regularly cycled between raging torrents
and dry creek beds. As a result, the Ozark Plateau
attracted only a relatively small population of hardy pioneers: folks willing to live in near isolation, and to get by
on food and goods found or made locally. As the decades
passed, their language retained old-fashioned words like
"sallet" for salad, and "critter" for creature (meaning animal); they made their own entertainment just as they made
their own clothes, getting together on Saturday nights to
play jigs and reels little changed from the colonial era.

As you'll see on this Ozarks drive, much has changed
in modern times, but some things have stayed the same.
The route begins in the university city of Fayetteville, the
center of one of the fastest growing metropolitan areas in
the South, and stops at important Civil War sites on the
way to quirky, picturesque Eureka Springs, a town
crowded with historic buildings. You'll visit the beautiful

Buffalo National River, the Ozark National Forest, and one of America's most famous highways before turning south to Mountain View. Here a unique state park offers a glimpse of the Ozarks' pioneer past, and a tour through Blanchard Springs Caverns reveals some of the most spectacular underground scenery in the country.

❶ Fayetteville *(Chamber of Commerce 501-521-1710 or 800-766-4626)* wraps around the campus of the **University of Arkansas** *(501-575-2000)*, which itself centers on **Old Main** *(Arkansas Ave.)*, an 1875 structure whose twin towers have symbolized the college experience for generations of graduates. Downtown, the **Washington County Courthouse** *(College and Center Sts.)*, a 1905 building of hand-cut native stone, is one of the city's emblems; take a peek inside at the World War I-themed lobby mural. The adjacent Romanesque 1897 **Old County Jail** is worth a look for its crenellated stone corner towers. A few blocks north, the 1853 **Headquarters House Museum** *(118 E. Dickson St. 501-521-2970. Mon., Thurs., and Sat., living history tours by appt.; adm. fee)* is one of Fayetteville's signifi-

cant buildings, having served as headquarters for both Union and Confederate forces during the 1863 Battle of Fayetteville; it's now furnished with items reflecting the antebellum period. Vintage airplanes crowd a World War II-era wooden hangar at the **Arkansas Air Museum** *(Drake Field, off Ark. 71 at 4290 S. School Ave. 501-521-4947. Adm. fee)*, which features craft from a biplane barnstormer to a modern Huey helicopter.

Cooper Barn at Shiloh Museum of Ozark History, Springdale

A few miles west of Fayetteville, **Prairie Grove Battlefield State Park** *(14262 US 62. 501-846-2990. Adm. fee for museum and buildings tour)* preserves part of the site of the last major Civil War clash in northwestern Arkansas. On December 7, 1862, Confederate forces heading northward were forced to withdraw when they ran short of ammunition after a bloody but indecisive battle. Several historically important structures—a schoolhouse, a church, a blacksmith shop, and a sorghum mill, among others—

have been moved from the surrounding area to the park, which uses them to interpret not only the battle but the Civil War's devastating consequences for the region's civilian population.

Following US 71B north from Fayetteville, be sure to stop in Springdale at the **Shiloh Museum of Ozark History** *(118 W. Johnson Ave. 501-750-8165. Closed Sun.)*, one of Arkansas's most rewarding small museums. Exhibits focus on regional heritage, including the timber, fruit, and poultry industries, as well as Native Americans, the Civil War, and the railroad era. Outside you'll find several significant and well-restored buildings, including an 1870s doctor's office, a fine old barn, and an outhouse from the 1930s.

❷ **Bentonville** may be best known as the home of one of the most amazing business success stories of the 20th century. You'll learn all about it at the **Wal-Mart Visitors Center** *(105 N. Main St. 501-273-1329. March-Oct. Mon.-Sat., Nov.-Feb. Tues.-Sat.)*, where interactive displays recount the phenomenal expansion of the discount chain under the leadership of its folksy but single-minded founder Sam

View from Mount Judea, off Scenic 7 Byway

Walton. On display in Walton's original variety store are his desk and the old pickup truck he continued to drive even after he'd made his first (and second and third…) billion.

Retrace your path and continue to Rogers, from which US 62 leads northeast to **Pea Ridge National Military Park**★ *(15930 US 62. 501-451-8122. Adm. fee)*, site of one of the largest Civil War engagements west of the Mississippi River. Often called "the battle that saved Missouri for the Union," the clash that erupted on March 7 and 8, 1862, saw Union forces turn back a Confederate thrust aimed at retaking St. Louis; two Rebel generals died during the fighting. Displays and audiovisual presentations in the Visitor Center tell the story of the battle, and a 7-mile driving route leads past interpretive displays. The tour highlight is a reconstruction of Elkhorn Tavern, which survived the fighting but burned and was rebuilt soon afterward.

Farther east on US 62, country music shows, motels, and souvenir shops dominate the outskirts of ❸ **Eureka Springs**★ *(Chamber of Commerce, US 62. 501-253-8737 or 800-638-7352)*, but at its center is one of Arkansas's most

131

important links to earlier times. The entire downtown area is listed on the National Register of Historic Places, its sometimes tortuous streets lined with splendid Victorian buildings. Stop by the **Eureka Springs Historical Museum** (95 S. Main St. 501-253-9417. April-Dec. daily, Jan.-March Tues.-Sat.; adm. fee) for an overview of the town's intriguing past.

In the late 19th century, "healing" waters were big business, and Eureka's many springs made it a boom-town, offering "the balm of life" to soothe all manner of illnesses. When the boom times passed, the town slept quietly for decades, until artists and hippie types rediscovered it in the 1960s, creating an idiosyncratic atmosphere that still prevails. ("In Eureka, people are entertained by one another's eccentricities, rather than appalled," a resident said recently.)

Pick up a walking tour brochure at the Chamber of Commerce or the historical museum, and use the trolleys or your feet to explore (traffic can be vexing at times). Among the many worthwhile stops: the ornately decorated **Rosalie House** (282 Spring St. 501-253-7377. Adm. fee), built by a wealthy, local businessman in the 1880s; the attractively restored **Bank of Eureka Springs** (70 S. Main St. 501-253-8241); the 1891 **Queen Anne Mansion** (207 Kingshighway. 501-253-8825. Adm. fee); and the 1886 **Crescent Hotel** (75 Prospect St. 501-253-9766), constructed of local limestone on a hilltop overlooking the city. Three miles west of downtown, **Thorncrown Chapel** (12968 US 62. 501-253-7401. Closed Jan.-Feb.; donation) is a must-see for anyone interested in contemporary design. This modest glass-and-wood structure, created by Fayetteville architect E. Fay Jones, stands as one of the most honored buildings of our time; it's one of the reasons Jones was awarded the Gold Medal of the American Institute of Architects in 1990.

Stop by the **Saunders Memorial Museum** (113-115 E. Madison St. 870-423-2563. Mid-April–Oct. Mon.-Sat.; adm. fee) in Berryville to see a huge collection of firearms, from fancy dueling pistols to military weapons to revolvers owned by the likes of Billy the Kid and Annie Oakley. In addition to the guns, the museum displays a varied collection of objects gathered during the world travels of its wealthy founder, businessman C. Burton Saunders, including furniture, wood carvings, textiles, silver, and clothing.

From Berryville, take Ark. 21 south to the tiny hamlet of ❹ **Boxley** and the **Buffalo National River** ★★ (Headquarters, 402 N. Walnut St., Harrison. 870-741-5443), one of the finest free-flowing streams in mid-America—and a marvelous setting for outdoor adventures from canoeing to hiking to camping to swimming to simply enjoying

A National First

Many of Arkansas's once free-flowing rivers have been lost to dams, to the regret of those who prefer canoeing and smallmouth bass fishing to water-skiing and fishing for large-mouth bass and imported trout. The White River and its North Fork, and the Ouachita, Caddo, and Cossatot Rivers all have been partially inundated by reservoirs in recent decades. The Buffalo River, one of the finest natural areas in the South, was saved only after years of bitter conflict and controversy between dam proponents and conservationists. In 1972 the Buffalo became America's first official national river, its pristine beauty protected for all time from a fate as just another sprawling mountain lake. Rent a canoe, grab a paddle, and see for yourself what all the fighting was about.

some of the most beautiful scenery in the Ozarks. Serious exploration of the Buffalo would require several days: The park section stretches for more than 130 miles from near its headwaters to its confluence with the White River. Spring high water brings challenging canoeing on the upper reaches, while the calmer flow downstream from US 65 is good for beginners. Check with local outfitters (the National Park Service headquarters in Harrison can provide a list) or rangers for current floating conditions. If you'd rather stay on dry land, the park offers several hiking trails.

At Boxley, take Ark. 43 north to **Lost Valley,** where a 2.1-mile loop trail leads upstream along Clark Creek to an overlook of shallow caves that once sheltered Native

133

Floating on the Buffalo National River

Americans. Turn eastward on Ark. 74 to **Steel Creek,** with camping and a great swimming hole beneath towering bluffs. At **Pruitt,** north on Ark. 7 from Jasper, you'll find a ranger station and another hiking trail.

Ark. 7 south of Jasper enters the main body of the **Ozark National Forest★** *(Supervisor's office, 605 W. Main St., Russellville. 501-968-2354. Office closed weekends),* whose six sections cover more than a million acres of northwestern and west-central Arkansas. This stretch of the highway, a section of **Scenic 7 Byway★,** has been listed by travel magazines countless times as one of America's top scenic drives. With its far-reaching panoramas it fully merits the honors it has received—though after spending time in the

Ozarks you might be hard pressed to choose it above some other equally deserving routes. While admiring the beauty of these hills, take geological note of their flat-topped outline: The Ozarks weren't pushed up through folding and faulting like some mountains, but comprise an "eroded plateau," lifted in one piece and then dissected over millions of years by the power of rivers.

Turn back north to Harrison on Ark. 7, and take US 62 east to Yellville, where a short side trip on Ark. 14 south leads to **Buffalo Point,** another access location for the Buffalo River, with cabins, camping, swimming, hiking trails, and nearby canoe rentals. About 5 miles north lies the ghost town of **Rush** *(Rush Rd., off Ark. 14),* which boomed to a population of more than 5,000 after zinc ore was discovered in the 1880s. Today the place that caused such a "rush" is just a scattering of picturesque wooden buildings in the forest, a reminder that the hills and the river weren't always as peaceful and calm as they are now.

Working a lathe at Ozark Folk Center State Park

Back on US 62, continue east to Flippin and loop north on Ark. 178 to **Bull Shoals Lake** *(U.S. Army Corps of Engineers 501-425-2700)* and **Bull Shoals State Park** *(River Run Rd. 870-431-5521),* both offering campsites and nationally renowned fishing: primarily for bass in the lake and trout in the cold waters of the White River below the dam. The fishing is good, too, for the majestic bald eagles that congregate in the area in winter.

Following Ark. 5 south from Mountain Home leads to the ➎ **Wolf House** *(870-499-9653. Mid-April–mid-Oct. Mon.-Sat.; adm. fee),* believed to have been built as early as 1816 and possibly the oldest two-story log structure in the state. This rustic dogtrot house (incorporating a breezeway through the ground floor) once served as a courthouse; its furnishings include items from Arkansas's territorial and early statehood days.

Where Ark. 5 crosses the White River at Calico Rock, it becomes the Forest Service's 26-mile **Sylamore Scenic Byway** *(Ranger District office 870-269-3228),* a lovely drive through a typical Ozark forest of oak, hickory, sycamore, dogwood, and maple. Wildflower season begins in March with early bloomers like bloodroot and hepatica, while in September the scarlet leaves of black gum herald the coming of bright fall foliage colors.

At Allison, turn west on Ark. 14 to **Blanchard Springs Caverns**★★ *(870-757-2211. April-Oct. daily, Nov.-March Wed.-Sun.; fee for tours. Reservations recommended for tours)*, a cave system not nearly as well known as its extraordinary beauty deserves. Caves are common in the soft limestone of the Ozarks, and Blanchard ranks not only as the best in the region but as one of the best in the country.

Operated by the U.S. Forest Service, Blanchard Springs Caverns offers tours along the **Dripstone Trail,** which passes through the upper part of the cave, past an astounding variety of speleothems (the technical name for formations such as stalactites and stalagmites); the longer (1.2 miles), more strenuous tour along the **Discovery Trail** *(Mem. Day–Labor Day only)* covers a younger section that has fewer formations but provides the opportunity to see close-up how an underground river has shaped the caverns.

Just beyond the cave entrance is Blanchard Springs itself, where the stream that carved the caverns rushes out of the rocky bluff. A bit farther on you'll find North Sylamore Creek, a perfect Ozark stream with clear water and tall bluffs, irresistible on a hot summer day. If the water is a bit crowded here, a hiking trail paralleling the creek will help you find a private swimming hole all your own.

South of Allison on Ark. 9, the little town of ❻ **Mountain View**★ *(Chamber of Commerce 870-269-8068)* owns a reputation among folk-music lovers disproportionate to its size. Fans of old-time music crowd the courthouse square for the annual **Arkansas Folk Festival**★ the third weekend in April, when folk, bluegrass, and gospel groups take the stage and jam sessions spring up anywhere a picker and a fiddler get together. On weekend evenings in summer, informal concerts attract locals and visitors alike.

It's not just the Ozarks' musical heritage that's preserved at the nearby **Ozark Folk Center State Park**★ *(Off Ark. 5. 870-269-3851. April-Oct.; adm. fee).* Here you'll find a deliberate and organized effort to keep some of the traditional mountain crafts alive—a place where spinning, woodcarving, basketry, blacksmithing, dollmaking, and other folksy arts are demonstrated for visitors, and passed on from old masters to a new generation. You can buy many of the items you see made here at the gift shop, and sample country cooking in the Folk Center's restaurant. Musicians play mountain tunes in the craft area during the day and in the theater each evening, when dancers of all ages take the stage for jig dancing and clogging.

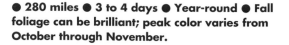

● 280 miles ● 3 to 4 days ● Year-round ● Fall foliage can be brilliant; peak color varies from October through November.

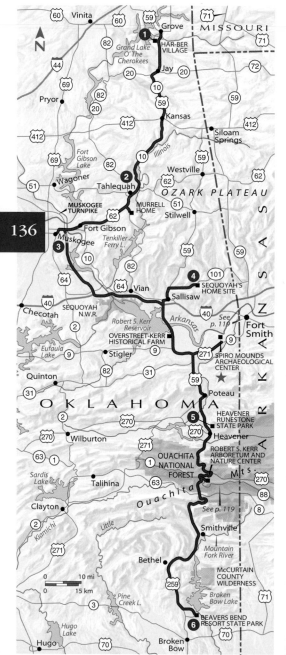

The land explored by this drive is not the Oklahoma of popular imagination: You'll see no vast prairie or rolling plains, oil-rich cities or western big skies. Instead, much of the route follows twisting two-lane highways over the Ozark and Ouachita mountains, through dense forests of oak and pine. This region is the extremity of America's great eastern woodland; beyond, rainfall decreases; the trees get scrubbier; and grassland begins to predominate. Historic sites dot the drive, including several related to Oklahoma's Native American legacy. Many rivers in the area have been dammed to create huge recreational lakes; for those who prefer natural streams, though, the famed Illinois River still offers fine canoeing for much of its length. And in places, scenic vistas reward the traveler with spectacular panoramas of some of the prettiest country in the central United States.

The drive begins near the Missouri border, heading south to the varied historic attractions around Muskogee. After following the Arkansas River Valley downstream, it pauses at Spiro Mounds, an important prehistoric Indian archaeological site. Then it's south again into the rugged Ouachita Mountains, finishing at Beavers Bend, one of the state's finest state parks.

On the shore of the winding Grand Lake O'The Cherokees near Grove lies one of Oklahoma's most unusual museums. ❶ **Har-Ber Village** *(Har-Ber Rd., W of US 59.*

918-786-6446. March–mid-Nov.; donation) was founded in 1968 by the wealthy owner of a trucking company and today comprises more than 100 buildings filled with all manner of antiques and historic items. This grab bag of the past ranges from tractors and wagons to guns and musical instruments; the collection is so extensive that nearly everyone will find something of interest. Household items include early washing machines, glassware, furniture, and many objects (fluting irons, sock knitters, kraut cutters) you may not have known existed. Some of the buildings along the paved pathway are original, moved here and restored, while others are reconstructions. One houses military items, another old buggies and stagecoaches, a third Indian artifacts, and so variously on. The presentation is a bit kitschy, but there's unquestionably a lot to see.

The Illinois River rises in Arkansas, flowing west and south through Oklahoma for nearly 70 miles before becoming lost in the waters of upper Tenkiller Ferry Lake. Its usually gentle rapids make it a good choice for families or beginning canoeists, and places such as Sparrow Hawk Mountain provide fine scenery along the way. Several access points are located on Okla. 10, and rental firms offer trips starting at just a few hours in length. For more information and a list of outfitters, contact the **Oklahoma Scenic Rivers Commission** *(Okla. 10, just N of Tahlequah. 918-456-3251 or 800-299-3251).*

❷ **Tahlequah** *(Tourism Council 918-456-3742 or 800-456-4860)* has long been the capital of the Cherokee Nation, the Native American people forced to leave their southeastern homeland in the 1830s during the relocation known as the Trail of Tears. The **Cherokee Heritage**

Mileage sign in Grove

137

Historic church at Har-Ber Village, near Grove

Illinois River, near Tahlequah

Center★ *(Willis Rd. 918-456-6007. May–Labor Day daily, Feb.-April and Labor Day–Dec. Tues.-Sat., closed Jan.; adm. fee)* presents the tribe's history in four venues: Exhibits in the Cherokee National Museum recount the journey to Indian Territory and the strong sense of family that helped the nation endure. Tsa-La-Gi Ancient Village *(guided tours mid-May–Labor Day)* is a re-created settlement of the period before Europeans arrived in North America, with living history demonstrations of basketry, cooking, pottery, and other everyday skills. Adams Corner Rural Village depicts the Cherokee lifestyle of the late 19th century, with costumed interpreters in a general store, church, one-room school, and other buildings typical of a small town. The Tsa-La-Gi Theater *(July–mid-Aug. Mon.-Sat.; fee)* tells the story of the Trail of Tears in dramatic form.

Costumed frontiersmen, Fort Gibson Historic Site

Not far away, the **Murrell Home** *(Okla. 82. 918-456-2751. April–Labor Day Wed.-Sat., call for winter schedule)* was built about 1845 by a well-to-do white merchant, George M. Murrell, who married a Cherokee woman, the daughter of a prominent family and the niece of the tribe's principal chief. "Hunter's Home," as Murrell called his house, is a two-story frame structure reminiscent of the mansions of his native Virginia; now under restoration, it's furnished with items interpreting Cherokee history of the antebellum era.

The U.S. Army established Fort Gibson in 1824 to try to keep the peace between the Osage and the Cherokee who had recently settled in the former tribe's traditional territory. Later, the post served as an administrative center for Indian "removal" and as a Union stronghold during the Civil War. **Fort Gibson Historic Site** *(907 N. Garrison Ave., Fort Gibson. 918-478-4088. Adm. fee)* comprises structures dating from the mid-1840s, including the old post hospital, barracks, and commissary, as well as reconstructions of the stockade, bakehouse, and living quarters for troops, who were once paid seven dollars a month. Exhibits recount the post's history from its establishment to its abandonment in 1890.

❸ **Muskogee** *(Tourism Bureau 918-684-6363)* took its name from the Muscogee Nation (called Creek by European settlers), one of the Five Civilized Tribes who inhabited the southeastern United States until forced to move to Indian Territory in the early 19th century; the others were the Seminole, Cherokee, Chickasaw, and Choctaw. The **Five Civilized Tribes Museum** *(Agency Hill on Honor Heights Dr. 918-683-1701. Adm. fee)* presents historical items of all these peoples—from farm tools to musical instruments, clothing, and jewelry—telling the story of their forced emigration and resettlement. An upstairs gallery houses works by noted Native American artists such as Jerome Tiger and Willard Stone. The museum's 1875 building originally housed the Union Indian Agency, a federal body comprising the government's superintendents of the five nations.

An extensive collection of Indian art and artifacts is also displayed at **Ataloa Lodge** *(2299 Old Bacone Rd. 918-683-4581. Mon.-Fri., or by appt.; adm. fee)*, on the campus of Bacone College. The works, both historic and modern, include pottery, textiles, sculpture, and paintings. In Muskogee War Memorial Park rests the **USS *Batfish*** *(3500 Batfish Rd., near Port of Muskogee. 918-682-6294. Mid-March–mid-Oct. Wed.-Mon., mid-Oct.–Nov. Fri.-Sun.; adm. fee)*, a much decorated warship that sank 14 enemy vessels in the latter part of World War II. If you're not too claustrophobic, you'll enjoy a tour of the control room, torpedo room, and crew's quarters of the 312-foot-long sub.

Located just south of I-40 near Vian, **Sequoyah National Wildlife Refuge** *(918-773-5251)* is one of Oklahoma's most popular areas for wildlife observation, especially birdwatching. Encompassing more than 20,000 acres on Robert S. Kerr Reservoir at the confluence of the Arkansas and Canadian Rivers, the refuge's 6-mile auto-tour route passes through mixed woodland and agricultural fields. Depending on the time of year, you may see bald eagles, snow geese and other waterfowl, and a variety of songbirds. From spring through fall look for the beautiful scissor-tailed flycatcher, Oklahoma's state bird.

Creek Council House

Located in Okmulgee, 45 miles southwest of Muskogee via US 62, the **Creek Council House Museum** *(106 W. 6th St. 918-756-2324. Tues.-Sat.)* is well worth a side trip for anyone interested in Native American history. The two-story brick building was constructed in 1878 by the Creek (Muscogee) Nation to serve as tribal capitol after its members were forced to leave their homeland in Georgia and Alabama. The two bodies of the Creek Legislature, the House of Kings and House of Warriors, met in upstairs rooms. Exhibits of artifacts, jewelry, clothing, and government documents tell the story of the Creek people from the era before European colonization to settlement in Indian Territory to Oklahoma statehood in 1907.

Like the county in which it's located, the wildlife refuge was named in honor of Sequoyah, the revered Cherokee who in the early 19th century invented a syllabary that enabled speakers of Cherokee to write their native language. Sequoyah moved to Indian Territory from Arkansas in 1829; the rough-hewn log cabin he built then still stands at ❹ **Sequoyah's Home Site** *(Okla. 101, 10 miles NE of Sallisaw. 918-775-2413. Closed Mon.),* preserved within a larger structure that also displays some of his farming tools, his spinning wheel, a Cherokee-language typewriter, and exhibits on his life and Cherokee history.

South of Sallisaw on US 59, **Overstreet-Kerr Historical Farm** *(918-966-3396. Tues.-Sat.; adm. fee)* centers on an imposing-looking two-story house, built in 1895 for a local couple and their nine children. Furnished with period articles, the home is adjoined by outbuildings typical of a late 19th-century homestead. Operated as a museum farm, the 140-acre spread preserves historic breeds of livestock including Pineywoods cattle, Spanish goats, and Choctaw ponies and hogs.

Sequoyah's Home Site, near Sallisaw

At the US 59 intersection with Okla. 9/US 271, drive east on Okla. 9/US 271 a short distance to visit one of America's most significant prehistoric Indian sites. **Spiro Mounds Archaeological Center** ★ *(Spiro Mounds Rd. 918-962-2062. Wed.-Sun.; donation)* marks the location of a regionally dominant center of commerce and religion in the Mississippian Period of Native American culture. During Spiro's zenith, from about A.D. 850 to 1450, its position on the Arkansas River made it a natural hub for trade between the Plains Indians and the tribes of the Southeast.

Artifacts found here prove Spiro was a center of religious rituals connected with the "Southern Cult," as well as the site of hundreds of ceremonial burials. A small museum displays some of the region's enormous variety of artifacts, including tools, pottery, beads, and amazingly detailed effigies and pipes.

Near the small town of Heavener lies another kind of artifact, one as mysterious and controversial as it is massive. The focus of ❺ **Heavener Runestone State Park** *(Morris Creek Rd., off US 59. 918-653-2241)* is a 10-by-12-foot slab of rock with an inscription that some have identified as runic writing dating from A.D. 600 to 800. Supposedly translated as "Glome Dal," or Glome's Valley, the runes are claimed by true believers to prove that Scandinavian explorers visited the region hundreds of years before Columbus; professional archaeologists are unconvinced. If you'd like to have a look yourself, the stone lies in a pretty valley on the side of Poteau Mountain beneath tall stone bluffs.

Overstreet-Kerr Historical Farm

141

Heading south on US 59 and US 259, the route soon enters the **Ouachita National Forest** *(Choctaw Ranger District 918-653 2991)*, at 1.7 million acres the South's largest national forest, providing visitors dozens of campgrounds, recreation areas, and trails. Turn east on the **Talimena Scenic Byway**★ (Okla. 1) for a mountaintop drive featuring fine vistas of the forested Ouachita Mountains. In less than 2 miles you arrive at **Robert S. Kerr Arboretum and Nature Center** *(918-653-2991)*, where exhibits and self-guided trails provide an introduction to the Ouachitas environment. The byway continues another 30 miles to Mena, Arkansas (see Hot Springs and the Ouachitas drive, p. 119).

Back on US 259, the next section of the drive passes through wooded hills for the hour or so south to ❻ **Beavers Bend Resort State Park** *(Okla. 259A 580-494-6300)*, on the Mountain Fork River below Broken Bow Lake. Beavers Bend certainly ranks among the most appealing of Oklahoma's parks; its attractions include tall rock bluffs, walking trails, and a beautiful stream for canoeing, fishing, and swimming. The park's nature center is home to various wild critters from snakes to hawks and owls; the **Forest Heritage and Education Center** *(405-494-6597)* follows the development of forests and the timber industry from prehistory to modern times.

● **425 miles** ● **4 to 5 days** ● **Year-round, though winter winds can be bitter on the prairie.**

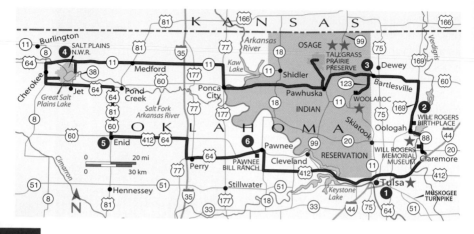

What does oil look like? If you think it's just black sticky gunk, keep your eyes open on this drive through north-central Oklahoma. You'll see that oil, through the alchemy of petrodollars, can take the shape of an art deco office building or a "palace on the prairie," a fabulous collection of Native American artifacts or an elegant garden—or even, in some cases, a whole town.

The legacy of oil wealth is only one part of this route, though. You'll also get acquainted with Will Rogers, the folksy comedian who made America laugh in the Roaring

Remingtons in the Gilcrease Museum

Twenties, and with Wild West showman Pawnee Bill. The drive traverses a vast tallgrass prairie nature preserve and later visits the Great Salt Plains, one of the most bizarre landscapes on the continent. And all along the way, museums both grand and modest tell the story of the transition from Indian Territory to modern Oklahoma.

❶ Tulsa★ *(Convention & Visitors Bureau, 616 S. Boston Ave. 918-585-1201 or 800-558-3311)* was founded in 1836 by the Lochapoka Band of Creek Indians, who had been forced from their homeland in Georgia and Alabama; the **Creek council oak tree** beneath which these settlers met still stands just south of downtown, near the Arkansas River at 18th Street and Cheyenne Avenue. Though the town was a ranching center before the turn of the century, oil discoveries caused a boom that led to Tulsa's claim by the 1920s to be the Oil Capital of the World. Perhaps the most visible reminders of that era are the city's historic art deco buildings; check with the Visitors Bureau for a guide to structures such as the **Boston Avenue Methodist Church** *(1301 S. Boston Ave.)*; the **Oklahoma Natural Gas Building** *(624 S. Boston Ave.)*, now the Noble Drilling Building; the **Philcade Building** *(511 S. Boston Ave.)*, known as the Amoco North Building; and **Tulsa Union Depot** *(3 S. Boston Ave.)*.

Tulsa cowboy

143

Ranking at the very top of Oklahoma's cultural assets, the **Gilcrease Museum**★★ *(1400 Gilcrease Museum Rd. 918-596-2700 or 888 655-2278. Closed Mon. Labor Day–Mem. Day; donation)* houses an important and extensive collection of

art of the American West (not just "Western art," as the museum takes pains to differentiate). Founded by wealthy oilman Thomas Gilcrease on the grounds of his estate, the museum displays grand landscapes by Thomas Moran, bronzes and paintings by Frederic Remington and Charles M. Russell, scenes of Indian life by George Catlin, as well as works by John Singer Sargent, James McNeil Whistler, John

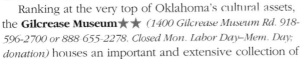

James Audubon (his magnificent painting of the wild turkey), George Caleb Bingham, and many, many others. Gilcrease was one-eighth Creek, and his interest in Native Americans also led him to amass a superb collection of pottery, baskets, clothing, jewelry, tools, and weapons.

The **Philbrook Museum of Art** ★ ★ (*2727 S. Rockford Rd. 918-749-7941 or 800-324-7941. Closed Mon.; adm. fee*) occupies an Italian Renaissance-style mansion built in 1927 by Waite Phillips, another wealthy oilman—one of a trio of brothers who came to Oklahoma from Iowa for the oil boom. (Frank and L.E. founded Phillips Petroleum in Bartlesville.) Waite Phillips donated his villa to Tulsa as an art museum in 1938; Philbrook also includes a modern wing added in 1990. The museum is known for Italian Renaissance paintings and sculpture, 19th- and 20th-century European and American paintings, African and Asian art, and an excellent collection of Native American paintings, baskets, and pottery. The 23-acre gardens include both naturalistic and formal plantings, originally intended to remind Waite and his wife, Genevieve, of the Tuscan hills they so loved.

Among Tulsa's other attractions: **Harmon Science Center** (*5707 E. 41st St. 918-622-5000. Tues.-Sun. in summer, Sat.-Sun. rest of year; adm. fee*) is full of hands-on exhibits and gadgets interpreting physics, weather, energy, and local geology. The collection of the **Gershon and Rebecca Fenster Museum of Jewish Art** (*1223 E. 17th Pl. 918-582-3732. Sun.-Thurs.*) includes Torah scrolls, ceremonial objects, a Holocaust education center, and photos documenting Jewish life in Oklahoma. The 800 acres of the **Oxley Nature Center** (*N. Sheridan Ave. and E. 36th St. N., in Mohawk Park. 918-669-6644*) include several short trails that cover a variety of habitats from woods to marsh.

In Claremore, the **J.M. Davis Arms & Historical Museum** (*333 N. Lynn Riggs Blvd. 918-341-5707. Donation*) devotes most of its considerable space to guns: thousands of them, from early European flintlocks to modern

Bedroom at Will Rogers Birthplace

144

sporting rifles to military machine guns. The Gallery of
Outlaw Guns displays firearms used by Bonnie Parker,
John Wesley Hardin, Pretty Boy Floyd, and Cole Younger;
nonlethal exhibits include musical instruments, Native
American artifacts, and stoneware.

When Will Rogers died in an Alaskan plane crash in
1935, his widow received telegrams of condolence from
Charlie Chaplin, Groucho Marx, and Franklin D. Roosevelt,
among many other admirers. You can see these and other
personal items at the fine **Will Rogers Memorial
Museum** ★ *(1720 W. Will Rogers Blvd. 918-341-0719 or 800-
828-9643),* situated on a hill on the outskirts of Claremore
and dedicated to the memory of the cowboy, vaudevil-
lian, comedian, writer, and movie star who never met a
man he didn't like. The expansive museum includes
Rogers' collection of saddles from around the world, and
rooms full of memorabilia from his careers as "The Cherokee Kid" in Wild West shows, as a performer in the
Ziegfeld Follies, and as a Hollywood star (and the highest
earning entertainer of his day). Museum theaters show
many of his popular movies.

Birdhouse at Woolaroc Ranch,
Museum, and Wildlife Preserve

145

Take Okla. 88 north to Oologah and continue a short
distance on US 169 to the ❷ **Will Rogers Birthplace**
(918-275-4201), the ranch where Rogers grew up and
learned to ride a horse and spin a rope. Also known as
the Dog Iron Ranch, today's 400-acre site operates as a
living history ranch, with longhorn cattle roaming outside
the two-story house where Rogers was born in 1879.

The story of ❸ **Bartlesville** *(Visitors Information Center
918-333-1800 or 800-364-8708)* is in large part the story of
Phillips Petroleum, which in turn is the legacy of Frank and
L.E. Phillips, pioneers of the Oklahoma oil industry. (Their
brother Waite, who had his own company until he sold out
to Frank, built Philbrook in Tulsa.) To experience a bit of
the oil-boom days, visit the **Frank Phillips Home** *(1107 S.
Cherokee Ave. 918-336-2491. Wed.-Sun.; donation),* a white-
columned, brick mansion just south of the city's center.
Completed in 1909 and extensively remodeled 21 years
later, the elegant house is full of furnishings and personal
items reflecting the tastes of Frank and his wife, Jane.

Downtown, the **Price Tower** *(6th and Dewey Sts. 918-
661-7471. Tours on Thurs. or by appt.; fee for tours)* was completed in 1956 to a Frank Lloyd Wright design. The
architect described the distinctive copper-and-glass office
building as "the tree that escaped the crowded forest"; as
was his usual practice, Wright also designed furnishings
to match the exterior style. On the first floor, the
Bartlesville Museum *(918-336-4949. Closed Mon.)* features

Oil pumper near Ponca City

rotating exhibits on art, architecture, science, and history.

To music lovers, the name Bartlesville is synonymous with the mid-June **OK Mozart International Festival**★ *(918-336-9900. Fee for performances)*, a highly praised series of concerts featuring the Solisti New York Orchestra and distinguished guest performers. Begun in 1985, the festival now comprises nine days and dozens of concerts.

Off Okla. 123 southwest of Bartlesville is another part of Frank Phillips's empire: **Woolaroc Ranch, Museum, and Wildlife Preserve**★ *(918-336-0307. May-Sept. daily, Tues.-Sun. rest of year; adm. fee)* was the oilman's country retreat, where he built a rustic lodge in 1927 and collected art and artifacts of the Old West. Today, Woolaroc (the name comes from "woods, lakes, and rocks") is part exotic-wildlife ranch and part museum complex. The eclectic collection in the main museum includes Native American items, mounted wildlife, and works by Remington and Russell. Also on the grounds are an exhibit on Oklahoma oil history, a Native American Heritage Center, and the original lodge, furnished as it was when Frank and Jane entertained guests such as Will Rogers and Harry Truman.

Backtrack to Bartlesville and follow US 60 west to Pawhuska, gateway to one of the state's—indeed, the nation's—finest and most important natural areas. The Nature Conservancy's **Tallgrass Prairie Preserve**★★ *(Via Kihekah St. 918-287-4803)* protects 37,000 acres of rolling terrain where grasses such as big bluestem can reach heights of 8 feet or more in late summer. Tallgrass prairie is among the most endangered environments in America; less than 10 percent of the original expanse of 142 million acres remains intact. By introducing bison and regular controlled burning to the preserve, the Nature Conservancy hopes to reestablish the naturally functioning ecosystem that existed when the early Osage roamed the land. In addition to a thriving herd of bison, as you drive or walk the trails here you may see prairie chickens, coyotes, deer, or any of dozens of species of wildflowers.

Ponca City *(Tourism Authority 580-767-8888 or 800-475-4400)* is home not only to one of Oklahoma's most magnificent houses, but to a sensational tale that reads like the plot of a juicy best-seller. E.W. Marland, who at one time controlled 10 percent of all the oil being produced in the world (his company eventually evolved into Conoco), set out in 1925 to build a home patterned on a palace he'd visited in Italy. By the time he was finished, his "Palace on the Prairie" had 55 rooms, 43,000 square feet, and was an awe-inspiring showplace of limestone, wood paneling, wrought iron, brass, gold leafing, and crystal. In the meantime, his first wife had died; Marland then married her niece, who was also his adopted daughter. The couple barely had time to move into their castle, however, before Marland lost all his money to J.P. Morgan in what would be considered today a hostile takeover…and that's just part of the story. To learn the rest, and to see a house that cost nearly 5.5 million dollars, visit the **Marland Estate Mansion**★ *(901 Monument Rd. 580-767-0420. Adm. fee)*, a spectacular monument to the glory that was the oil boom.

Marland once employed a third of all the workers in Ponca City, and in his heyday he donated land and money for many civic projects. One was the **Pioneer Woman Statue** *(701 Monument Rd. 580-765-6108)*, a 17-foot-high bronze depiction of a young mother and her son, symbolizing the hardiness and courage that Marland thought were missing in the flapper girls of his time. The adjoining museum is undergoing a major expansion, with new exhibits recounting the contributions of women in Oklahoma history; call for details on the re-opening.

Head north on US 77, west on Okla. 11, and south on Okla. 38 to tour the northern part of the ❹ **Salt Plains National Wildlife Refuge** *(580-626-4794)*, where you may see waterfowl, turkey, eagles, herons, or shorebirds—or, in spring and fall, sandhill and rare whooping cranes.

Returning to Okla. 11, continue west to Okla. 8 and take it south through Cherokee, following signs to the salt flat area of the refuge. Here in this vast expanse of dried mud topped with blindingly white salt, you may feel as if you've stepped out of your car onto the surface of a different planet. From April to mid-October, rock hounds and other curious visitors are allowed to dig for crystals of selenite, a type of gypsum that forms just below the surface. The small brownish crystals are quite common

Tom and Tony

Tom Mix was one of America's most celebrated silent-movie cowboys, featured in more than 300 shoot-'em-ups like *The Arizona Wildcat* and *Riders of the Purple Sage*. When talkies came in, Mix went out—but he capitalized on his movie fame by becoming a highly paid circus performer. The *Tom Mix Ralston Straight Shooters* radio show featured several different actors playing the star, which conveniently allowed the program to continue for ten years after Mix's death in a car wreck in 1940. In **Dewey,** where Mix once served as a deputy marshal, the **Tom Mix Museum** *(721 N. Delaware St. 918-534-1555. Closed Mon.; donation)* displays all sorts of Mix memorabilia, from fancy saddles to photographs to the trinkets sold to *Straight Shooter* fans on the radio show. And not least, there's a full-size re-creation of Tom's long-time pal, Tony the Wonder Horse.

147

and not really worth anything, but they're fun to find and make nice souvenirs of a visit to this exotic terrain.

Take US 64 back east, then south to ❺ **Enid** *(Chamber of Commerce 580-237-2494 or 800-299-2494)*. The sound of real Burlington Northern Santa Fe trains passing by outside provides an appropriate soundtrack for the **Railroad Museum of Oklahoma** *(702 N. Washington St. 580-233-3051. Closed Mon.; donation)*, located in a restored Santa Fe freight depot. Train buffs from all over the country have donated to the collection of memorabilia here, which includes china and silver service from famous passenger trains, more than 100 switch lanterns, signs from old depots, and a 60-foot model train layout.

Pretty Government Springs Park is adjoined by the **Museum of the Cherokee Strip** *(507 S. 4th St. 580-237-1907. Closed Mon.)*. Exhibits here interpret the history of the area of northwestern Oklahoma once known as the Cherokee Outlet, or Cherokee Strip, which was opened to white settlement on September 16, 1893. Indian artifacts, pioneer tools, and photos are combined in well-presented displays that tell the story of the largest of all the state's land runs. In the adjacent **Humphrey Heritage Village** stand several historic buildings relocated to the park, including the 1893 land office where settlers filed their claims.

Marland Estate Mansion, Ponca City

In Perry, the **Cherokee Strip Museum** *(2617 W. Fir St. 580-336-2405. Closed Sun.-Mon. and first 2 weeks of Jan.)* looks at turn-of-the-century Noble County, with re-created doctor's and dentist's offices, household utensils from early farm life, and personal items from local families.

On a hilltop just west of Pawnee stands a rock house completed in 1910 by Gordon W. Lillie, better known as the entertainer "Pawnee Bill." After a period touring with "Buffalo Bill" Cody, Lillie in 1888 started his own Pawnee Bill's Historic Wild West show: "A Grand and Glorious Gathering of the World's Most Famous Hero Horsemen, Indians, Cowboys, Arabs, Mexicans...." The show featured his wife, a trick-shot artist. The ❻ **Pawnee Bill Ranch** *(Off US 64. 918-762-2513)* offers tours of the Lillies' home, a museum with many of their costumes and personal items, and a bison herd.

Return to Tulsa via Okla. 18 and US 412.

● **400 miles** ● **4 to 6 days** ● **Year-round**

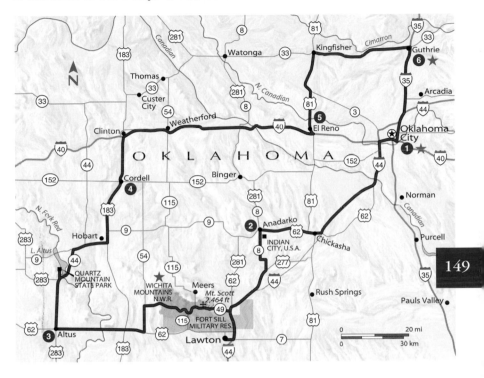

Oklahoma City's eclectic array of museums makes a busy beginning for this loop through the southwestern part of the state; from the Old West to spacecraft, there's something in OKC for all ages and interests. Once away from the capital, the drive heads across the plains—at times on lonesome rural highways—to visit a center of Native American culture, an excellent wildlife refuge, one of the state's most attractive parks, and a museum dedicated to America's "Mother Road," fabled Route 66. The last stop is Guthrie, Oklahoma's first capital, where the expansive historic district comprises literally hundreds of 19th-century buildings.

Speaking of busy beginnings: ❶ **Oklahoma City**★ *(Convention & Visitors Bureau 405-297-8912 or 800-225-5652)* was born in a feverish rush on April 22, 1889, when the area known as Indian Territory was opened for settlement in the first of the area's great land runs. In a matter of hours, 10,000 people took up residence where a day earlier there had been only a Santa Fe railroad station and a couple of shacks. A good place to learn about Oklahoma's past is the **Oklahoma State Museum of History** *(2100 N.*

State Capitol

Lincoln Blvd. 405-521-2491. Closed Sun.), part of the Oklahoma State Capitol Complex. A 19th-century bison-hide tepee and a restored 1870s stagecoach highlight exhibits that begin with prehistoric Indians and continue through the Civil War (state law requires the museum to maintain separate Union and Confederate rooms), territorial days, statehood, and into the oil-boom era of the early 20th century. After visiting the museum, walk over to the **State Capitol** *(405-521-3356. Tours Mon.-Fri.)* to see a plaza of Indian tribal flags and the now-capped Petunia Number One oil well, which once pumped crude from below the statehouse.

Not far from the capitol are two other worthwhile historical sites: **Harn Homestead and 1889ERS Museum** *(313 N.E. 16th St. 405-235-4058. Tues.-Sat.; adm. fee)* includes a 1904 Queen Anne-style farmhouse, an 1897 schoolhouse, and other houses and outbuildings. The elegant 1903 **Overholser Mansion** *(405 N.W. 15th St. 405-528-8485. Closed Mon.)* was built by one of the city's most prominent early businessmen; with a French château-style exterior, it features stained glass and fine wood paneling inside.

You'll find some of Oklahoma City's best attractions close together northeast of the downtown area, near the junction of I-44 and I-35. **Omniplex**★★ *(2100 N.E. 52nd St. 405-427-5461 or 800-532-7652. Adm. fee)* is actually an assemblage of several museums under one (very large) roof. Exactly what belongs to whom may be more than the average visitor cares to know; the important thing is that there's an awful lot of interesting stuff here. You can see a 1929 Pullman parlor car, a collection of watercolors by the great ornithologist-artist George M. Sutton, a 54-square-foot dollhouse, and a Japanese meditation garden…and that's just for openers. Kids can explore a spacious science center with hands-on exhibits, and all ages will enjoy the planetarium and **Air Space Museum**★, with antique biplanes, a full-size model of a lunar excursion module, flight trainers, and all sorts of historic aircraft and technology from the intervening years. Also on the site are the **Red Earth Indian Center** *(405-427-5228),* with galleries of Native American art and artifacts, and the **International Photography Hall of Fame and Museum** *(405-424-4055),* with changing displays and a huge photomural of the Grand Canyon.

Don't be fooled by the name of the excellent **National Cowboy Hall of Fame and Western Heritage Center**★ *(1700 N.E. 63rd St. 405-478-2250. Adm. fee);* even those with no interest in broncos and dogies will enjoy a visit to this museum-gallery complex. Art by Remington, Russell, Bierstadt, and lesser known contemporaries fills several rooms, along with works by modern painters and sculptors following in their boot steps. A children's interactive gallery allows kids to dress in Western clothes and visit a bunkhouse. Other areas focus on the West in movies and music, exhibiting prizes such as the Winchester Model 92 rifle that John Wayne used in several films.

The **45th Infantry Division Museum** *(2145 N.E. 36th St. 405-424-5313. Closed Mon.)* packs a lot of military memorabilia into its rooms; even the grounds outside display tanks, artillery, and aircraft. Weapons range from the American Revolutionary era through the Persian Gulf war; one room is dedicated to the great cartoonist Bill Mauldin, who served in the 45th Infantry in World War II.

Other attractions in the same general area that may appeal include the **Oklahoma Firefighters Museum** *(2716 N.E. 50th St. 405-424-3440. Adm. fee),* the **National Softball Hall of Fame** *(2801 N.E. 50th St. 405-424-5266. Adm. fee),* and the admirable **Oklahoma City Zoological Park** *(2101 N.E. 50th St. 405-424-3344. Adm. fee).*

From Oklahoma City, follow I-44 and US 62 southwest to ❷ **Anadarko,** a regional center of Native American culture. Bronze busts of more than three dozen noted figures are displayed on an outdoor walk at the **National Hall of Fame for Famous American Indians** *(851 E. Central Blvd./US 62. 405-247-5555).* Chief Joseph of the Nez Perce, athlete Jim Thorpe, and entertainer Will Rogers are among those commemorated here. Next door, the **Southern Plains Indian Museum** *(715 E. Central Blvd. 405-247-6221. Closed Mon. Oct.-May; adm. fee)* has displays on clothing, music, religion, and other aspects of Plains Indian life; the adjacent crafts center has a good selection of work by Indian artists. Just south of town on Okla. 8, **Indian City, U.S.A.** *(Okla. 8. 405-247-5661 or 800-433-5661.*

James Earle Fraser's "The End of the Trail," National Cowboy Hall of Fame and Western Heritage Center, Oklahoma City

Meers Store

While you're visiting Wichita Mountains National Wildlife Refuge near Lawton, take time to drive a few miles north on Okla. 115 to the tiny—in fact, almost nonexistent—hamlet of Meers. Although it boomed during a turn-of-the-century gold rush, Meers is now down to a handful of buildings, the most famous of which is the **Meers Store** *(Okla. 115. 580-429-8051).* Formerly a doctor's office, newspaper office, and general store, it's now a restaurant specializing in hamburgers made with beef from longhorn cattle. Lively, cluttered, and colorful, the venerable spot is worth a visit whether you're eating or just looking.

152

Adm. fee), comprises authentic re-creations of dwellings of seven different Indian tribes, including a large Wichita grass lodge and Caddo wood-and-mud houses.

Lawton *(Chamber of Commerce 580-355-3541 or 800-872-4540)* is home to Fort Sill, where the constant *thoomp* of big guns reminds visitors that this is the headquarters for Army and Marine artillery training. The **Fort Sill Museum** *(437 Quanah Rd. 580-442-5123)* recounts the colorful history of the post, which was founded in 1869 to keep the peace between white settlers from Texas and Plains Indians, and since 1911 has been the country's major gunnery school. More than 25 of the museum's buildings date back to the 1870s and contain exhibits and historic weapons; outside, the Cannon Walk displays artillery pieces including "Atomic Annie," which fired the first nuclear shell in 1953.

The **Museum of the Great Plains** *(601 N.W. Ferris Ave. 580-581-3460. Adm. fee)* features a fine collection relating to the part of the country once called the "Great American Desert," from a mammoth skull to a 1926 Baldwin steam locomotive. Exhibits include a re-created small-town storefront, items from an Indian store in Anadarko, and a big, complicated-looking peanut-threshing machine. The adjacent **Percussive Arts Society Museum** *(701 N.W. Ferris Ave. 580-353-1455. Adm. fee)* will bring out the latent drummer in anybody. Marimbas, steel drums, chimes, and xylophones are among the percussion instruments on exhibit; a trap set used by famed drummer Shelly Manne occupies a place of honor.

Take Okla. 49 west from Lawton through **Wichita Mountains National Wildlife Refuge** ★ *(Visitor Center, Okla. 49 and Okla. 115. 580-429-3222. Visitor Center closed Tues.),* where rugged, rocky hills rise over plains, woods, and lakes, comprising more than 60,000 acres of diverse habitat. Bison, elk, and longhorn cattle are easily seen from refuge roads, along with prairie dogs, white-tailed deer, and a wide variety of birds. You can experience quite a bit of the area from your car (don't miss the drive to the top of Mount Scott), but for a more solitary experience the refuge offers several miles of hiking trails.

Cow skull at Indian City, U.S.A., near Anadarko

Follow Okla. 54 south to US 62 and turn west to ❸ **Altus,** where the **Museum of the Western Prairie** *(1100 N. Hightower St. 580-482-1044. Closed Mon.; donation),* located in a regionally appropriate dugout-style building, looks at life in the southern Great Plains: the nomadic Native Americans who once roamed here, the white settlers who faced an arid environment with great extremes of weather, and the agriculture and ranching that dominate today. North of Altus via US 283 and Okla. 44, **Quartz Mountain State Park** *(Okla. 44A. 580-563-2238)* borders 6,260-acre Lake Altus, and includes the reddish granite bulk of Quartz Mountain itself—like the hills of the Wichita refuge to the east, worn down from much greater elevation by hundreds of millions of years of erosion. The view from the top is worth the effort of hiking.

Continue north now on Okla. 44 and 9 and US 183, stopping in ❹ **Cordell** just long enough to admire the 1910 **Washita County Courthouse** *(100 Main St./Okla. 152)*, with its copper dome and white columns surely one of the most striking public buildings in Oklahoma.

Dedicated in 1926, Route 66 (see sidebar p. 154) soon became known as "America's Main Street," or even, as John Steinbeck wrote, "the Mother Road." Symbolizing the nation's push westward

Schoolmarm interpreter, Chisholm Trail Museum in Kingfisher

to the promised land of California—as well as the newfound freedom of the automobile—Route 66 ran 2,440 miles from Chicago to Santa Monica before the growth of interstates transformed it into country roads and side streets. Clinton's **Route 66 Museum** *(2229 W. Gary Blvd. 580-323-7866. Closed Mon. Labor Day–Mem. Day; adm. fee)* takes visitors back to the days when highway travel was an adventure, with souvenirs, photos, road signs, and antique vehicles, all presented to a nostalgic soundtrack; the featured tune, of course, is Bobby Troup's classic "Get Your Kicks On Route 66."

Drive east on I-40 to ❺ **El Reno,** where you may be momentarily confused by a Big 8 motel sign on old Route 66 reading "Amarillo's Finest"; it's left over from the movie *Rain Man,* in which El Reno stood in for the Texas town. Take time to visit the **Canadian County Historical Museum** *(300 S. Grand St. 405-262-5121. Wed.-Sun.),* which includes the 1906 Rock Island depot, a restored 1892 hotel, and local artifacts from Indian times to railroading days.

Guthrie color

Get Your Kicks

Oklahoma had more miles (more than 400) of the original Route 66 than any other state, and recent years have seen increased efforts to preserve historic attractions along "America's Main Street." One of the most famous is the beautiful **Round Barn** *(Okla. 66. 405-396-2398)*, a restored 1898 building at Arcadia, just northeast of Oklahoma City. Another, near Foyil (north of Claremore), is **Totem Pole Park** *(Okla. 28A. 918-342-9149)*, where a folk artist named Ed Galloway built several strange structures, including a weirdly decorated concrete cone sometimes called "the world's largest totem pole." One of the best guides to the old highway is *Route 66: The Mother Road*, by Michael Wallis.

Follow US 81 north to Kingfisher and the **Chisholm Trail Museum** *(605 Zellers Ave. 405-375-5176. Closed Mon.; donation),* named for its location on the celebrated trail used to drive cattle north from Texas to markets in Kansas. Old farm machinery, vehicles, clothing, guns, and wildlife displays make up just part of the collection; around back are several restored buildings, including a log cabin owned by Adaline Dalton, four of whose 13 children decided that crime, after all, did pay and formed the notorious Dalton Gang.

Take Okla. 33 east to **6** **Guthrie**★ *(Visitors Bureau 405-282-1948 or 800-299-1889),* a mandatory stop for any history buff. Like Oklahoma City, Guthrie sprang to life on the day of the April 22, 1889 land run. It served as the territorial and state capital until 1910, when, after a bitter campaign, voters chose to move the seat of government to Oklahoma City. As progress passed it by, Guthrie kept its 19th- and early 20th-century buildings intact; the town now has the largest contiguous urban historic district on the National Register of Historic Places.

For many visitors, the gem of Guthrie is the **State Capital Publishing Museum**★ *(301 W. Harrison Ave. 405-282-4123. Closed Mon.).* Housed in a massive 1902 brick building is an entire turn-of-the-century printing plant, complete with presses, typesetting machines, and a beautifully preserved sales office. The *State Capital* was once one of Oklahoma's most successful newspapers, but, like Guthrie, went into decline (in its case, a fatal one) when Oklahoma City took over as capital.

Exhibits at the **Oklahoma Territorial Museum** *(406 E. Oklahoma St. 405-282-1889. Closed Mon.; donation)* cover events leading up to the 1889 land run, continuing through the period before statehood was attained in 1907. Boomers (those who pushed for opening of Indian lands for nonnative settlement), Sooners (who sneaked across the line before the official start of land runs), and ordinary homesteaders were all part of that era, along with outlaws and cheats who jumped claims or sold land they didn't own. Also part of the museum is the restored 1902 **Carnegie Library** next door. Andrew Carnegie believed his money would have been better spent on books than the elaborate fireplaces and fancy dome.

Just down the street, the **Scottish Rite Masonic Temple**★ *(900 E. Oklahoma Ave. 405-282-1281. Mon.-Fri.;*

adm. fee) is, simply speaking, a wonder. Completed in 1929, the Greek Revival-style edifice combines limestone, marble, crystal, huge columns, elegant woodwork, and decorative painting into 268,000 square feet of fanciful architecture and design. As you wander around pondering what it must have cost, one thought comes to mind: It's a good thing they got it finished before the stock market crashed.

Return to Oklahoma City south on I-35.

Celebrating '89er Day in Guthrie

TEXAS

Texas Tourism Division General information *512-462-9191.*

Department of Parks and Wildlife State parks and campground information *512-389-8950.* Hunting and fishing license information *512-389-4820.*

Department of Transportation Road conditions *800-452-9292.*

LOUISIANA

Louisiana Department of Culture, Recreation and Tourism General information *800-633-6970.*

Department of Wildlife and Fisheries Hunting and fishing license information *504-765-2800.*

Office of State Parks State parks and campground information *504-342-8111.*

Louisiana Bed & Breakfast Association B&B listings *504-346-1857.*

MISSISSIPPI

Mississippi State Tourism Division General information *800-927-6378.*

Department of Wildlife, Fisheries, and Parks State park and campground information *800-467-2757.* Hunting and fishing license information *601-364-2040.*

Bed & Breakfast Association of Mississippi B&B listings *800-217-2588.*

ARKANSAS

Arkansas Department of Parks and Tourism General information *501-682-7777.* State parks and campground information *888-287-2757.*

Game and Fish Commission Hunting and fishing license information *800-364-4263.*

Highway and Transportation Department Road conditions *501-569-2227.*

Bed & Breakfast Association of Arkansas B&B listings *501-868-8905.*

OKLAHOMA

Oklahoma Tourism and Recreation Department General information *800-652-6552.*

Department of Public Safety Road conditions *405-425-2385.*

Department of Wildlife Conservation Hunting and fishing license information *405-521-4624.*

Parks and Resorts Department State parks and campground information *800-654-8240.*

HOTEL & MOTEL CHAINS

(Accommodations in all five states unless otherwise noted)

Best Western International *800-528-1234*

Budget Host *800-BUD-HOST* (except Miss. and Ark.)

Choice Hotels *800-4-CHOICE*

Clarion Hotels *800-CLARION* (except Miss.)

Comfort Inns *800-228-5150*

Courtyard by Marriott *800-321-2211*

Days Inn *800-325-2525*

Doubletree Hotels and Guest Suites *800-222-TREE* (except Miss.)

Econo Lodge *800-446-6900*

Embassy Suites *800-362-2779* (except Miss.)

Hampton Inn *800-HAMPTON*

Hilton Hotels *800-HILTONS* (except Miss.)

Holiday Inns *800-HOLIDAY*

Howard Johnson *800-654-2000*

Hyatt Hotels and Resorts *800-233-1234* (La. and Tex. only)

Marriott Hotels Resorts Suites *800-228-9290*

Motel Six *800-466-8356*

Quality Inns-Hotels-Suites *800-228-5151*

Radisson Hotels Intl. *800-333-3333* (except Miss. and Ark.)

Ramada Inns *800-2-RAMADA*

Red Roof Inns *800-843-7663* (except Okla.)

Ritz-Carlton *800-241-3333* (Tex. only)

ITT Sheraton Hotels & Inns *800-325-3535* (except Miss.)

Super 8 Motels *800-843-1991*

Travelodge International Inc. *800-255-3050* (except Ark.)

Utell International *800-223-9868*

ILLUSTRATIONS CREDITS

Photographs in this book are by Danny Lehman, except the following: 8 Buddy Mays/Travel Stock; 15 Robb Kendrick; 31 Steven C. Wilson/ ENTHEOS; 42-43 Richard Reynolds; 44 Bill Ballenberg; 45 Texas Dept. of Commerce photo by Richard Reynolds; 47 Gail Mooney; 58 Blair Pittman; 79 C.C. Lockwood; 86-87 Bob Sacha; 91 Bob Clemenz; 93, 94 Mike Clemmer; 95 Dan Guravich; 105 Steve Wall; 107 William Albert Allard, NGP; 111 Sandy Felsenthal; 122 Hank Wilson; 123 Sheila Yount/Arkansas Parks & Tourism; 124 Ed Cooper Photo; 130-131, 133 Matt Bradley; 155 Jim Argo/Stock Options.

NOTES ON AUTHOR AND PHOTOGRAPHER

MEL WHITE is a freelance writer living in Little Rock, Arkansas, and specializing in travel and natural history. He has written for several Book Division publications and is a frequent contributor to NATIONAL GEOGRAPHIC TRAVELER, for which he has covered destinations ranging from Amazonia to the Swiss Alps.

The National Geographic has utilized photographer DANNY LEHMAN's talents throughout the world and has published 19 of his projects, including *National Geographic's Driving Guides to America, The Southwest*. His more than 20-year career has taken him from the remote mountains of New Guinea to the interior of Alaska. He lives in Santa Fe with his wife, Laurie, and two boys, Daniel and Jonathan.

Index

Composition for this book by the National Geographic Society Book Division. Printed and bound by R.R. Donnelley & Sons, Willard, Ohio. Color separations by Digital Color Image, Pensauken, New Jersey. Paper by Consolidated/Alling & Cory, Willow Grove, Pennsylvania. Cover printed by Miken Companies, Inc. Cheektowaga, New York.

Library of Congress Cataloging-in-Publication Data

White, Mel, 1950-
    Texas, and Louisiana, Mississippi, Arkansas, and Oklahoma / by Mel White ; prepared by the Book Division, National Geographic Society.
       p.   cm. — (National Geographic's driving guides to America)
    Includes index.
    IBSN 0-7922-3433-2
    1. Texas—Tours. 2. Louisiana—Tours. 3. Arkansas—Tours. 4. Oklahoma—Tours. 5. Mississippi—Tours. 6. Automobile travel—Texas—Guidebooks. 7. Automobile travel—Arkansas—Guidebooks. 8. Automobile travel—Oklahoma—Guidebooks. 9. Automobile travel—Louisiana—Guidebooks. 10. Automobile travel—Mississippi—Guidebooks. I. National Geographic Society (U.S.). Book Division. II. Title. III. Series.
    F396.W59 1997
    917.604'43—dc21   97-40688
                                     CIP

Visit the Society's Web site at www.nationalgeographic.com